Profit Extraction

Tax-efficient choices for getting money out of your company

Advisors & Publishers

© 2005 Indicator Limited.

We have made every effort to ensure that the information contained

in this book reflects the law as at August 1, 2005.

The male pronoun has been used throughout. This is simply to avoid cumbersome language

and no discrimination or bias is intended.

No part of this publication may be reproduced or transmitted in any form or by any means

or stored in any retrieval system without permission.

ISBN 0-9548140-5-3

Third Edition - E3P1

© 2005 Indicator Limited.

Every effort has been made by Indicator Limited to ensure that the information given is accurate and not misleading,

but Indicator Limited cannot accept responsibility for any loss or liability perceived

to have arisen from the use of any such information. Only Acts of Parliament and Statutory Instruments

have the force of law and only the courts can authoritatively interpret the law.

INTRODUCTION

Profit. You've made the profit but which is the most tax-effective way to get it out of your company? In this book you will find 19 tax-efficient profit extraction methods. Choose the one (or combination of several) that best suits your personal circumstances.

Extraction. In fact, you can just take a salary from your company. That's where we start in Part 1. However, we then go on show you other ways to extract profit that may be more tax effective. For each of these methods we tell you, in simple language, what's involved, the tax consequences for you and your company and whether there are any VAT implications. We also provide you with a worked example and finish off with advantages and disadvantages (pros and cons) of using each method. To make it easier to draw comparisons between the methods we've stuck to the same structure for each part of this book.

How to use this book. This book can be used as a source of reference to dip into as and when required. However, it's best used to help you plan the most tax-effective way of extracting profit from your company in the future. We show you how to do this in the Conclusion part of the book, which is also where we compare each of the methods. Armed with this information you will be able to devise a simple strategy to withdraw profit and pay the least amount of tax. Profit Extraction won't result in a zero tax bill every time - but it will certainly lead to considerably more of your profit staying in your pocket.

In this edition. The book has been revised and updated to include the latest tax rates and thresholds for 2005/6. We've also added a complementary CD-ROM which is home to a powerful tool kit. This takes the examples in the book that one step further by actually allowing you to personalise profit extraction methods with you own figures; then rank and compare them. For each method the before-and after-tax cost is shown together with graphic representations to make the numbers even easier to follow. This toolkit even takes into account the new Corporation Tax rate on profits extracted by way of dividends and the recent change to the taxation of childcare vouchers.

Martin Attis
Editor
Indicator Advisors and publishers

September 2005

CONTENTS

TABLE OF CONTENTS

PART 4 INTEREST

PART 5 RENT

© Profit Extraction, Indicator

TABLE OF CONTENTS

TABLE OF CONTENTS

© PROFIT EXTRACTION, Indicator

TABLE OF CONTENTS

PART 11   FREE ACCOMMODATION

PART 12   CHILDCARE

© PROFIT EXTRACTION, Indicator

TABLE OF CONTENTS

PART 16

SELLING TO THE COMPANY

PART 17

USING A COMPANY PENSION FUND

TABLE OF CONTENTS

TABLE OF CONTENTS

© PROFIT EXTRACTION, Indicator

PART 21   TIMING

PART 22   APPENDICES

TABLE OF CONTENTS

Profit Extraction

Salary

SECTION 1: METHOD

© Profit Extraction, Indicator

WHAT DO WE MEAN BY SALARY?

By salary we mean the regular pay that you receive as the manager, director or Chairman of your company. Other forms of remuneration, such as having the company pay for your medical insurance or having the use of a company car, will be discussed later.

In other words, salary is a reward for the effort of people who work for the company, rather than those who just own a stake in the company i.e. the shareholders. So if you are just a shareholder and do no actual work for the company you can't strictly receive a salary. You can, however, be paid a dividend (see Part 3).

HOW SHOULD YOU WITHDRAW SALARY?

Your salary can be paid in cash, by cheque or as a transfer to your bank account from the company's account. The method of making the payment is just like paying any other employee. Your company takes off any income tax and NI due and then pays the balance (the net amount) over to you; subject to some special rules on directors' NI (see Part 2).

In credit. The company doesn't actually have to pay the net salary out of its bank account into yours; it can instead make an accounting entry to credit your director's current account with the net amount due. This leaves the cash in the company until you need to draw it out. When you draw on your current account with the company there is no more tax to pay.

WHAT IS THE MAXIMUM SALARY YOU CAN HAVE?

Unrestricted. In principle you can withdraw as much pay as you want. There is no upper limit on the amount you pay yourself, but there is a legal minimum called the National Minimum Wage. This will apply to you if you are legally treated as a worker employed by your company but may not if you only act in an official capacity as a company director or company secretary.

Not unimportant. Obviously, the more salary you take the more tax you will pay, so the level of salary is important if you prefer not to pay too much tax.

On the other hand, withdrawing no pay at all is not ideal either, because it can restrict the amount of tax-deductible pension contributions you can make and affect your future entitlement to certain Social Security benefits and the State Pension.

Your company will also benefit from you taking out some salary, as the pay you take will reduce profits and the amount of tax paid on them.

SECTION 2: YOUR COMPANY

IS SALARY TAX-DEDUCTIBLE FOR THE COMPANY?

Yes. The salary paid, is in principle, always deductible as it's an expense wholly and exclusively incurred by the company for the purposes of its trade.

Conditions. In order to deduct a director's salary as an expense against the company's profits, it must *first* be approved and voted on by the shareholders of the company. This can be done in advance by approving the service contract of the director. There may be only one shareholder: you, in which case you should ask the company secretary to record in the company's minute book the level of salary agreed for the year. If the salary is not approved, any money taken from the company should technically be treated as a loan until approved.

The *second* condition for the salary to be tax-deductible is that it must be paid within nine months of the end of the company's accounting period. If the company has a year-end of December 31, any salary due must be paid by September 30, 2005 to be set against the profits made in 2004.

The *third* condition is that the pay must not be excessive in relation to the work done. For example, paying a part-time employee £40,000 per year just for answering the telephone. The Taxman may argue that the reward does not reflect the work done, so the payment is not tax-deductible for your company.

WHAT IS THE NI COST?

There is employers' NI at 12.8% to pay on salary over £4,895 (or £94 a week).

DOES THE COMPANY HAVE TO DEDUCT TAX FROM YOUR SALARY?

Yes. As is the case with other employees, the company must deduct income tax and NI under the Pay-As-You-Earn (PAYE) system from the pay of directors and thus your own pay.

Risk. If you do not deduct income tax and NI from salary when it's due the Taxman can demand it from the company. He can look at the amounts paid in the previous six years and demand interest on the income tax and NI that was not paid on time, plus penalties for not operating a PAYE scheme correctly.

Example.

> *You withdraw gross pay of £2,000 per month. In simple terms, with tax due at 22% and NI at 11%, the net amount you are allowed to transfer to your private bank account is £1,340 (£2,000 x 67%). The company has to pay £916 (100% - 67% = 33% x £2,000 = £660 + employers' NI: 12.8% x £2,000 = £256) to the Taxman. The exact amount of tax due under PAYE will depend on the PAYE code in operation for the month in question.*

> *If you do not operate PAYE and transfer £2,000 to your private bank account each month you will be taxed as if you had received gross pay of £2,985 (£2,000/67 x 100). The company will have to pay the missing tax and NI on this plus interest for late payment, and a penalty which may be as much as 100% of the tax due.*

SALARY

DOES IT MATTER HOW MUCH SALARY IS PAID?

Probably. The amount of salary you withdraw from your company can affect the level of Corporation Tax (CT) your company will be subject to.

Reducing Corporation Tax. The rates of CT depend on the level of profits after deduction of expenses, such as salaries, as follows:

CORPORATION TAX	
TAXABLE PROFITS	**RATE OF CT**
0 TO £10,000	0% STARTING RATE
£10,001 TO £50,000	23.75% MARGINAL RATE
£50,001 TO £300,000	19% SMALL COMPANY RATE
£300,001 TO £1,500,000	32.75% MARGINAL RATE
OVER £1,500,000	30% LARGE COMPANY RATE

Example.

Your company has made taxable profits of £100,000 in the year ended March 31, 2004. It will owe Corporation Tax of: £100,000 x 19% = £19,000. If you draw a salary of £60,000 from the company the taxable profits are reduced to £40,000 and the Corporation Tax due is:

TAX RATE		£
STARTING RATE	£10,000 x 0%	0
MARGINAL RATE	£30,000 x 23.75%	7,125
TOTAL CT DUE		7,125

IR35 warning. If your company provides your personal services to other businesses it may be caught by the tax rules known as IR35, which have a substantial effect on the level of salary that must be drawn from the company. These rules are complicated so if you think your company may be caught by them you should seek professional advice.

SALARY

© PROFIT EXTRACTION, indicator

SECTION 3: YOU

SHOULD YOUR SALARY BE SHOWN ON YOUR TAX RETURN?

Yes. Your salary is income from an employment so you should complete the "Employment" pages on your tax return. If you receive a salary from more than one company you should complete a separate set of "Employment" pages for each company.

WHAT IS THE NI COST?

Your salary is subject to employees' NI at the following rates:

EMPLOYEES' NI	
SALARY	**2005/06**
FIRST £4,895	0%
NEXT £27,865	11% *(OR 9.4%)**
OVER £32,760	1%

*The lower rate of NI for the middle band of earnings is paid if you are a member of an approved company pension scheme that provides certain minimum benefits on retirement and you have "contracted out" of the State Earnings Related Pension Scheme (SERPS).

You do not pay NI on any salary paid after you reach state pensionable age, which is 65 for men and 60 for women born before April 6,1960.

There is no maximum Class 1 NI amount.

CAN YOU DEDUCT ANY EXPENSES FROM YOUR SALARY?

In order to deduct expenses from your salary the costs must be wholly, exclusively and necessarily incurred in the performance of your work. This is a very strict test and does not cover expenses incurred to put you in a better position to perform your duties, such as the cost of travelling to work.

Professional subscriptions. Members of professions may deduct the cost of fees and subscriptions paid to their professional bodies that they are required to belong to as a condition of their employment. The Taxman keeps a list of the approved bodies.

Business mileage. If you use your own car for business and the company pays you less than the tax-free rate (see Part 8) you can claim the difference.

All of these expenses should be claimed on the "Employment" pages of your tax return.

SALARY

AT WHAT RATE WILL SALARY FINALLY BE TAXED?

It depends. The rate at which you pay income tax on your salary depends on your total income during the tax year.

INCOME TAX RATES FOR EARNINGS IN TAX YEAR 2005/06	
TAXABLE INCOME	**TAX RATE**
FIRST £2,090	10%
NEXT £30,310	22%
ABOVE £32,400	40%

Tax-free. Your taxable income is your total income less the personal allowance, which is set at £4,895 for the tax year 2005/06. If you are aged over 65 your personal allowance is £7,090 for 2005/06.

PAYE code. Your salary should have most of the tax due deducted under the PAYE system before you receive it. However, if your total income has suddenly increased or the PAYE code used during the tax year was incorrect for any reason you may have some additional tax to pay based on your tax return.

This additional tax will be due to be paid on January 31 following the end of the tax year, which is also the final date for submitting your tax return. The additional tax due will be included within your PAYE code for the following tax year (say, 2006/07), as long as the amount due is less than £2,000. This means that you do not have to find the cash on January 31 to pay the tax due, as it will be collected from your salary in the next tax year. The catch is you have to submit your tax return early enough for this to be possible.

SALARY

© PROFIT EXTRACTION, indicator

SECTION 4: VAT

ARE THERE ANY CONSEQUENCES FOR VAT?

Withdrawing a salary from your company has no VAT consequences whatsoever.

However, if you invoice the company for your time, or your salary is paid to you through another agent, the VAT situation is different.

SECTION 5: EXAMPLE

This is an example of the tax related consequences of withdrawing salary from your company.

We first look at what the payment of the salary costs your company in net terms. We are taking into account the fact that the salary is tax-deductible for the company. We will then calculate the net amount that you will be left with as an individual after deduction of income tax and NI.

We have used the following assumptions:

Salary withdrawn	£50,000
Corporation Tax (CT) rate paid by the company	19% / 23.75%
Your highest personal tax rate	40%
Employers' NI rate on salary over £4,895	12.8%
Employees' NI rate between £4,895 and £32,760	11%

COMPANY'S TAX POSITION			
2005/06	**£**	**£**	**CT PAYABLE**
TAXABLE PROFIT IN THE COMPANY BEFORE DEDUCTION OF YOUR SALARY		70,000.00	13,300.00
GROSS SALARY WITHDRAWN	50,000.00		
EMPLOYERS' NI AT 12.8% ON £45,105 (£50,000 - £4,895)	5,773.44		
TOTAL SALARY COSTS		-55,773.44	
NET PROFIT AFTER SALARY*		14,226.56	1,003.80
CT SAVED BY PAYING THE SALARY	-12,296.20		-12,296.20
NET COST TO THE COMPANY (COSTS LESS CT SAVED)	43,477.24		

NET COST AS A PERCENTAGE OF THE GROSS SALARY	86.95%

*The first £10,000 of profit is taxed at 0%.

YOUR TAX POSITION			
2005/06	**£**	**£**	**%**
SALARY WITHDRAWN	50,000.00	50,000.00	100.00%
LESS PERSONAL ALLOWANCE	-4,895.00		
TAXABLE SALARY	45,105.00		
EMPLOYEES' NI £27,865 AT 11%	-3,065.15		
EMPLOYEES' NI £17,240 AT 1%	-172.40		
INCOME TAX AT 10% ON £2,090	-209.00		
INCOME TAX AT 22% ON THE NEXT £30,310	-6,668.20		
INCOME TAX AT 40% ON THE EXCESS OVER £32,400	-5,082.00		
TOTAL TAXES PAID		-15,196.75	30.39%
NET SALARY AVAILABLE TO SPEND		34,803.25	69.61%

SALARY

© PROFIT EXTRACTION, Indicator

SECTION 6: PROS & CONS

ADVANTAGES OF SALARY

1. Tax cautious. Most of the tax and NI for a given tax year will have been paid upfront under the PAYE system, meaning you don't have to find the money later.

2. Pension contributions. You can pay up to £300 (gross) per month into a stakeholder or personal pension scheme regardless of salary size. What a salary does do is push up the maximum amount of pension contribution you are allowed to pay into a personal pension scheme or a company scheme. If you have no salary one year you can use the salary of a previous year (within the last five) to base your salary contributions on. If you are near retirement age your salary can also maximise the amount of pension you will receive from a company pension scheme when you retire.

3. State benefits. If you receive a salary from the company you will be entitled to receive certain State benefits such as, Statutory Sick Pay, Statutory Maternity Pay and, since April 6, 2003, Statutory Paternity Pay and Statutory Adoption Pay. The NI contributions, which are payable on salary, entitle you to claim certain other State benefits should you become unemployed, bereaved or have a long-term illness. Also, if you pay the full rate of NI on your salary you will build up an entitlement to an increased State Pension when you reach retirement age.

DISADVANTAGES OF SALARY

1. NI. In addition to income tax, your gross salary will be subject to NI for both you as a private individual at 11% on a salary between £4,895 and £32,760 p.a. and 1% thereafter. For your company it's 12.8% on all your salary above £4,895 p.a.

2. Taxman's pocket. Income tax and NI must be deducted from your salary before you receive it under the PAYE scheme. This means you can't use the tax money elsewhere to make even more money before you pay the tax.

3. Restricted deduction of expenses. There are only a very few limited expenses which can be deducted from your salary income.

SALARY

Profit Extraction

Bonus

SECTION 1: METHOD

WHAT DO WE MEAN BY A BONUS?

A bonus is paid in addition to a salary. A bonus is a special reward for the work of employees or directors. How much you can afford to pay depends on how much profit the company has made.

Shareholders who supply the company with cash (by buying shares in the company) are rewarded with dividends (see Part 3) rather than bonuses. Many directors may also be shareholders, so it's always important to distinguish whether an amount paid to a director is a bonus or a dividend. The tax treatment is quite different.

HOW DO YOU AWARD YOURSELF A BONUS?

Minuted. The rules of most companies, the Articles of Association, require the company's shareholders to agree any remuneration paid to a director, usually by voting on a resolution approving the sum to be paid for the year at the Annual Generally Meeting (AGM). However, in practice, salary and bonuses are paid to directors before this meeting happens. If you are the only shareholder you should record, in the company's minute book, the level of bonus agreed for the year.

Entered. Your bonus can be paid in cash, by cheque or as a transfer to your private bank account from the company's bank account. A bonus may also be paid by transferring the ownership of an asset such as a car, to the director. You could leave your bonus within the company, so that the company credits the after-tax amount to your director's current account. The bonus is available to you to draw at any time you want and it's taxed just as if the company had given you a cheque on the date it's put into your director's current account. You subsequently draw your after-tax bonus from the company, as you need it.

DOES IT MATTER HOW BIG THE BONUS IS?

Unrestricted. In principle, you can withdraw as much profit by way of bonus as you want. It's counted as part of your total pay and there's no upper limit to this. Of course you cannot award more bonus than the company has made in profits.

Not unimportant. Obviously the larger the bonus the more tax you will pay, as your total income for the year will be higher. So the level of your bonus is important if you prefer not to pay too much tax. The payment of a large bonus also attracts a high NI cost for both you and the company.

Alternatives. The money paid as a bonus can often be taken out of the company in a different form, as discussed in the other parts of this book. If a large bonus is extracted from the company there will be less money available to reward directors in other, possibly more tax-efficient, ways.

BONUS

© PROFIT EXTRACTION, Indicator

SECTION 2: YOUR COMPANY

IS A BONUS TAX-DEDUCTIBLE FOR THE COMPANY?

Yes. In principle a bonus is always deductible for the company, as it's an expense wholly and exclusively incurred by the company for the purposes of its trade.

Deductible in which financial year? One of the great things about a bonus is that it's tax-deductible in the financial year it relates to and not the year in which it's awarded, i.e. not the year in which the shareholders' meeting decided on it.

Example.

> In 2004 your company made a £50,000 profit. Whilst finalising the accounts during 2005, you decide to award a £20,000 bonus. This bonus is still deductible for the financial year 2004, even though it's not been awarded until 2005. This means that, for the financial year 2004, your company will be taxed on £30,000.
>
> A bonus is therefore an ideal way to reduce the taxable profit of the company even when the financial year-end has passed.

Condition. For the bonus to be tax-deductible it must be paid or credited to the director's current account within nine months of the end of the company's year-end.

Example.

> If the company draws up its accounts to December 31, 2005, any bonus due for 2005 must be paid or credited by September 30, 2006 to be set against the profits made in the 2005 set of accounts.

Not excessive. In practice it's very rare for the Taxman to challenge the size of a bonus paid to a director. However, he will look to see if the bonus is "excessive", meaning the total amount of remuneration (which includes salary, bonuses and other benefits) is disproportionate to the actual work done, or the responsibilities of the job. If the Taxman successfully argues that the bonus paid was excessive he will prevent the company from deducting the cost from profits.

Investment company. If yours is an investment company, the Taxman may not allow it to deduct all its management expenses, which include directors' salaries and bonuses, from profits. An investment company is one that exists to hold and manage investments rather than carry on a trade.

WHAT IS THE NI COST?

The company has to pay employers' NI on your bonus at the rate of 12.8%. For example, a £10,000 bonus means the company has another £1,280 (12.8% x £10,000) to pay out.

DOES THE COMPANY HAVE TO DEDUCT ANY TAX AND NI?

Yes. As is the case with salary (see Part 1), the company must deduct income tax and employees' NI under Pay-As-You-Earn (PAYE) from the bonus, and pay over the employers' NI due on it.

Timing. The tax and employees' NI must be deducted from the bonus on the earliest date that the bonus is:

(1) Voted on by the shareholders; (2) the director becomes entitled to receive the payment; (3) the bonus is credited to the director's current account, even if he cannot immediately draw it from the company; or (4) the bonus is actually paid.

The income tax and NI deducted, plus the employers' NI must then be paid over to the Taxman by the next 19th of the month, as part of the normal PAYE process.

Special employees' NI rules. The NI deductions are normally restricted by an "Upper Earnings Limit" applying to the period for which salary is paid, monthly or weekly. This can lead to less NI being deducted if a director is paid a low salary and a high bonus once a year.

Example.

The director receives a monthly salary of £2,000 and a bonus of £26,000 on January 31, 2006. The NI paid and due for 2005/06 is:

	EARNINGS	DIRECTOR'S NI	EMPLOYERS' NI
January 2006	£28,000.00	£508.13	£3,531.78
Other months	£2,000.00 x 11 = £22,000.00	£175.13 x 11 = £1,926.43	£203.79 x 11 = £2,241.69
Total	£50,000.00	£2,434.56	£5,773.47
Annual NI due		£3,237.55	£5,773.44
Additional NI to be paid at end of tax year		£802.99	£Nil*

*Amount due is less than £1 so it's ignored.

To avoid such an underpayment the NI paid for directors must be reviewed at the end of each tax year in relation to the annual thresholds, and any additional NI paid two weeks after the end of the tax year.

Mistakes. The company should deduct all the NI due from your bonus before you receive it. If a mistake has been made in the NI calculations the Taxman will ask the company to pay any additional NI due. When you reach state retirement age, which is 65 for men and 60 for women born before April 6, 1960, no further NI should be deducted from your bonus or salary.

© PROFIT EXTRACTION, Indicator

BONUS

SECTION 3: YOU

SHOULD YOUR BONUS BE SHOWN ON YOUR TAX RETURN?

Yes. Your bonus is part of your income from employment so you should complete the "Employment" pages on your tax return.

When? A bonus is taxable in the year in which it is awarded or paid out. This is not necessarily the same year as the company gets a tax deduction for it.

Example.

> In the calendar year 2005 your company makes a £50,000 profit. During the finalising of the accounts you decide to award a £20,000 bonus in June 2006. That bonus will be deductible for your company in 2005, even though it has not been awarded until 2006. For its 2005 accounting year your company will be taxed on £30,000 (£50,000 - £20,000).
>
> However, you will not be taxed on your bonus until June 2006 (year of assessment 2006/07) because it was not awarded or paid out until then. This means it will go on your 2006/07 tax return.

How? The amount of your bonus should be included in the total figure of earnings from employment shown on the Form P60, which you should receive from the company by May 31 each year. To complete your tax return, copy the figures of pay and tax deducted from the P60 into the appropriate boxes on the tax return "Employment" pages. You do not have to copy over the amount of employees' NI you have paid on your bonus and salary.

Exceptions. If it's a special non-taxable bonus, such as a payment from a staff suggestion scheme, you do not have to include it on your tax return.

WHAT IS THE NI COST?

Bonus payments are subject to employees' NI at the following rates:

EMPLOYEES' NI RATES	
TOTAL ANNUAL EARNINGS	**2005/06**
AMOUNT UNDER £32,760	11% *(OR 9.4%)**
AMOUNT OVER £32,760	1%

The lower rate of NI for the middle band of earnings is paid if you are a member of an approved company pension scheme that provides certain minimum benefits on retirement and you have "contracted out" of the State Earnings Related Pension Scheme (SERPS).

An employee does not pay NI contributions on any bonus paid after they reach state pensionable age.

The company should deduct all the NI due from your bonus before the net amount is paid to you. If a mistake has been made in the calculations, the Taxman will ask the company to pay any additional NI due.

BONUS

CAN YOU DEDUCT ANY EXPENSES FROM A BONUS?

Yes, to a limited extent. The expenses that can be deducted from a bonus payment are the same as those that can be deducted from salary, (see Part 1).

AT WHAT RATE WILL YOUR BONUS FINALLY BE TAXED?

It depends. Your bonus is taxed just like your salary, so the final amount of tax you pay on your bonus will depend on the level of your total income for the year in which the bonus is awarded or paid, as explained in Part 1. The full amount of tax due under PAYE should have been deducted by the company and paid over to the Taxman before you receive the net amount.

However, if the PAYE code used was incorrect for any reason, the tax due on your bonus may be more than the tax deducted under PAYE. In this case there will be some additional tax due, which will show up when you submit your tax return. If this sum is less than £2,000 the Taxman will adjust your PAYE code for the next tax year to collect the tax due gradually with the tax for that year. He can only do this if your tax return is submitted early. If you wait until January 31, the Taxman will not have time to adjust your PAYE code, which is sent out in February, to be used from April 5.

If the additional tax due is more than £2,000 it must be paid by January 31, following the end of the tax year, which is also the final date for submitting your tax return.

© PROFIT EXTRACTION, Indicator

SECTION 4: VAT

ARE THERE ANY CONSEQUENCES FOR VAT?

No. Withdrawing a bonus from your company has no VAT consequences. Bonuses paid to employees and directors are not subject to VAT, so the bonus payment needs no specific VAT treatment.

BONUS

SECTION 5: EXAMPLE

This is an example of the tax-related consequences of your company paying you a bonus.

We examine the net cost of the bonus for your company, taking into account the fact that it is tax-deductible for the company. We then calculate the net amount that you will be left with as an individual after deduction of income tax and NI.

We have used the following assumptions:

Tax year	2005/06
Salary already withdrawn	£36,000
Proposed bonus	£15,000
Corporation Tax (CT) rate paid by the company	23.75%
Bonus fully taxable at your highest income tax rate of	40%
Employers' NI rate on bonus	12.8%
Employees' NI rate on bonus	1%

EXAMPLE 1. IF YOU ARE ALREADY A 40% TAXPAYER.

COMPANY'S TAX POSITION			
2005/06 TAX YEAR	**£**	**£**	**CT PAYABLE**
TAXABLE PROFIT IN THE COMPANY BEFORE DEDUCTION OF YOUR BONUS		30,000.00	4,750.00
GROSS BONUS WITHDRAWN	15,000.00		
EMPLOYERS' NI (12.8% ON £15,000)	1,920.00		
TOTAL COST OF BONUS		-16,920.00	
NET PROFIT AFTER BONUS (THE FIRST £10,000 OF PROFIT IS TAXED AT 0%)		13,080.00	731.50
CT SAVED BY PAYING SALARY	-4,018.50		-4,018.50
NET COST TO THE COMPANY (COSTS LESS CT SAVED)	12,901.50		

NET COST AS A PERCENTAGE OF THE GROSS BONUS	86.01%

YOUR TAX POSITION			
2005/06 TAX YEAR	**£**	**£**	**%**
GROSS BONUS		15,000.00	100%
INCOME TAX (AT 40% ON £15,000)	-6,000.00		
EMPLOYEES' NI (AT 1% ON £15,000)	-150.00		
TOTAL TAXES PAID		-6,150.00	41%
NET BONUS AVAILABLE TO SPEND		8,850.00	59%

© PROFIT EXTRACTION, Indicator

BONUS

EXAMPLE 2. IF YOU ARE ONLY PAYING TAX AT 22%.

COMPANY'S TAX POSITION			
2005/06 TAX YEAR	**£**	**£**	**CT PAYABLE**
TAXABLE PROFIT IN THE COMPANY BEFORE DEDUCTION OF YOUR BONUS		30,000.00	4,750.00
GROSS BONUS WITHDRAWN	15,000.00		
EMPLOYERS' NI *(12.8% ON £15,000)*	1,920.00		
TOTAL COST OF BONUS		-16,920.00	
NET PROFIT AFTER BONUS *(THE FIRST £10,000 OF PROFIT IS TAXED AT 0%)*		13,080.00	731.50
CT SAVED BY PAYING SALARY	-4,018.50		-4,018.50
NET COST TO THE COMPANY *(COSTS LESS CT SAVED)*	12,901.50		
NET COST AS A PERCENTAGE OF THE GROSS BONUS	86.01%		

YOUR TAX POSITION			
2005/06 TAX YEAR	**£**	**£**	**%**
GROSS BONUS		15,000.00	100%
INCOME TAX *(AT 22% ON £15,000)*	-3,300.00		
EMPLOYEES' NI *(AT 11% ON £15,000)*	-1,650.00		
TOTAL TAXES PAID		-4,950.00	33%
NET BONUS AVAILABLE TO SPEND		10,050.00	67%

BONUS

SECTION 6: PROS & CONS

ADVANTAGES OF A BONUS

1. Unrestricted amount. You can withdraw as much as you want from your company by way of bonus as long as it's not excessive compared to the work done and the responsibility of the job.

2. Increased pension contributions. A bonus payment can be used to boost your earned income for a particular tax year, which is then used as the basis for your pension contributions for the next five years.

3. Clear loan account. If your director's loan account with the company is overdrawn, a bonus can be credited to that account and so bring it back into credit.

4. Reduced Corporation Tax. You can withdraw a bonus from your company up to nine months after the company's year end to reduce the taxable profits for that accounting year. This would even bring them into a lower Corporation Tax band.

5. Increased corporate losses. If the company makes a very small loss, paying a bonus can increase that loss, which may be set against profits the company made in the previous year and generate a repayment of Corporation Tax.

DISADVANTAGES OF A BONUS

1. Employees' NI. In addition to income tax, employees' NI must be deducted from your bonus at the rate of 11% up to £32,760 p.a. and 1% of NI is deducted from all bonuses paid if your earnings are already in excess of that upper threshold.

2. Employers' NI. The company must pay employers' NI at the rate of 12.8% on top of the bonus paid to you.

3. Tax paid in advance. Income tax and NI must be deducted from your bonus under the PAYE scheme, if it's a taxable bonus, before you receive the net amount.

4. No basis for lending. As a bonus is an irregular payment and is not guaranteed income, some lenders will not consider it part of your income as the basis for a mortgage or other loan.

5. No diversion. A bonus cannot easily be transferred to another person, such as a member of your family.

© PROFIT EXTRACTION, Indicator

Profit Extraction

Dividends

SECTION 1: METHOD

WHAT DO WE MEAN BY DIVIDENDS?

A dividend is a reward for the shareholders of the company for supplying the company with capital when they buy or "subscribe" for the shares. The shareholder does not have to work for the company to receive a dividend.

If a company has profits it can pay a dividend to its shareholders. A dividend payment is made to the shareholders of the company according to the number of shares that each particular shareholder holds. The level of the dividend is normally expressed as a number of pence per share.

HOW SHOULD YOU WITHDRAW A DIVIDEND?

A dividend may be paid annually or at more regular intervals such as quarterly. It can be paid in cash, by cheque or as a transfer to your private bank account from the company's account. Or you could leave it as a credit to you and draw it down when you need it.

Approval. The company directors decide on the maximum level of dividend that should be paid according to the profit figures shown in the company's annual accounts. They then recommend the suggested dividend figure to the shareholders who vote on whether to pay the recommended amount or a smaller figure. When this vote is recorded the dividend is said to be "declared". The shareholders cannot vote to pay a level of dividends higher than the figure recommended by the directors. There may be a gap between the date the dividend is declared and the date on which the dividend is actually paid to shareholders.

Interim and final. The directors' powers to recommend or to pay dividends are set out in the company's rules known as the "Articles of Association". Most small companies will use the standard rules known as Table A. These rules permit directors to pay interim dividends before the final dividend is declared.

IS THERE A LIMIT TO THE SIZE OF DIVIDENDS?

Out of profits. A company can pay a dividend if it's made a profit (that is not cancelled out by losses). The profit figure considered is that amount left after Corporation Tax has been deducted. The maximum dividend payable by the company is an amount equal to the profit after tax for the year, plus any profits made in earlier years that have not been paid out.

Maximum to shareholder. The maximum dividend you can receive as a shareholder depends on the proportion of the company's shares you hold. If you hold 100% of the type and class of shares for which that dividend is paid, you will receive 100% of that dividend. If there are other shareholders holding the same class of shares the total dividend payable is divided between all the shareholders with those shares.

Cash. It might not be a great idea to take all the profits as a dividend as the company may need to keep some of that money to invest in equipment or to assist in case of a crisis. The directors actually have a legal obligation to consider the cash needs of the company before they recommend a dividend.

© PROFIT EXTRACTION, Indicator

DIVIDENDS

SECTION 2: YOUR COMPANY

IS A DIVIDEND TAX-DEDUCTIBLE FOR THE COMPANY?

No. The dividend is paid out of the company's profits after the tax due has been deducted. The payment of dividends only affects the amount of tax the company pays if its profits are less than £50,000.

Minuted. When a dividend is declared, the Company Secretary must record the details in the company's minute book. The dividend should only be paid to shareholders included in the company's register of shareholders and who have paid the full amount due to the company for their shares.

WHAT IS THE NI COST?

None. There is no employers' NI on dividends.

SHOULD THE COMPANY DEDUCT TAX WHEN PAYING A DIVIDEND?

No. The company should not deduct tax when paying a dividend. The dividend payment is not a payment of earnings so it must not be included in payments subject to Pay As You Earn. Dividends are not subject to any NI.

Tax credit. Although no tax is deducted from the payment of a dividend, the shareholder does receive a dividend with a tax credit of one ninth of the net dividend attached. The shareholder is taxed on the gross amount of the dividend including the tax credit, but is able to use that tax credit to offset some or all of the tax due. The tax credit is not related to the Corporation Tax paid by the company.

Example.

> *The company pays a dividend of £1,000 to its shareholder. The shareholder receives £1,000 but is taxed on £1,111.11. That is dividend paid plus tax credit of 1/9 x £1,000 = £111.11.*

Dividend vouchers. The company must prepare a dividend voucher to give to each shareholder when the dividend is paid. The voucher must show the date the dividend is paid, the number of shares held, the net amount paid, the tax credit that attaches to the dividend and the gross amount of the dividend including the tax credit (see Appendix 1).

ANY RESTRICTIONS ON PAYING A DIVIDEND?

Illegal dividend. If the directors allow a dividend to be paid when there are not enough retained profits in the company to cover payment, the dividend will be treated as illegal. In this case the Taxman may treat the dividend payment as a loan to the shareholders which can create a further tax charge (see Part 6).

IR35. If your company provides your personal services to other businesses it may be caught by the tax rules known as IR35. In this case if the company pays out a large value of dividends in the same tax year in which it receives income subject to IR35, it might not have enough cash left to pay the additional income tax and NI due on the deemed salary.

DIVIDENDS

SECTION 3: YOU

SHOULD A DIVIDEND BE SHOWN ON YOUR TAX RETURN?

Yes. If you complete a tax return the total amount of dividends you receive during a tax year should be shown under "Income from UK savings and investments". You need to collect all the vouchers for dividends paid during the tax year and add up the figures of net dividend and gross dividend and tax credit. These three totals must be included under the sub-heading "Dividends".

CAN YOU DEDUCT ANY EXPENSES FROM THE DIVIDEND?

No. Expenses may only be deducted from earned income or rental income.

Pension contributions. As a dividend is not earned income it is ignored when calculating the maximum pension contribution that may be paid into a company pension scheme or a personal pension scheme. Although the cash received as a dividend payment may be used to pay a pension contribution, the permitted level of that contribution is calculated according to earned income such as salary and bonuses received in that tax year or in an earlier tax year (within the previous five years).

WHAT IS THE NI COST?

None. There is no employees' NI on dividends.

AT WHAT RATE WILL A DIVIDEND BE TAXED?

It depends. The amount of tax due on the dividends you receive depends on the level of your other income received in the same tax year. The income tax rates that apply to dividends received in 2005/06 are:

TAXATION OF DIVIDEND INCOME	
TAXABLE INCOME	TAX RATE
ON FIRST £32,400	10%
ABOVE £32,400	32.5%

Imagine all your taxable income is piled up. The lower parts of the pile are taxed at the lower rates. When the pile of income exceeds £32,400 for 2005/06 the higher tax rates apply. Dividend income is always treated as if it sits on top of your pile of income.

Your taxable income is your total income less the personal allowance of £4,895 for the tax year 2005/06. If you are aged over 65 your personal allowance is £7,090 for 2005/06.

DIVIDENDS

© PROFIT EXTRACTION, Indicator

Example.

In the tax year to April 5, 2005 you receive dividends totalling £40,000, and no other income. The income tax due is calculated as follows:

	TAXABLE INCOME (£)	TAX DUE (£)
DIVIDEND	40,000	
TAX CREDIT (1/9 x £40,000)	4,444	
GROSS DIVIDEND	44,444	
PERSONAL ALLOWANCE	-4,745	
TAXABLE DIVIDEND	39,699	
INCOME TAX AT 10% (ON THE FIRST £32,400)		-3,240
INCOME TAX AT 32.5% (ON THE NEXT £7,299)		-2,372
OFFSET TAX CREDIT		4,444
TAX PAYABLE		1,168

Tax refunds. If you have no other income in the tax year, such that the dividend you receive is covered by your tax-free personal allowance, you cannot reclaim the tax credit on the dividend. It is better to receive a small salary or bonus to use up the personal allowance so that the tax credit attached to the dividend can then be offset against income tax.

SECTION 4: VAT

© PROFIT EXTRACTION, Indicator

ARE THERE ANY CONSEQUENCES FOR VAT?

None. Withdrawing a dividend from your company has no VAT consequences. The fact you are a shareholder of your company does not mean that as an individual you become liable to VAT on the money you withdraw as a dividend from your company. Dividends paid to shareholders are also not subject to VAT so the dividend payment does not require an invoice to be raised.

DIVIDENDS

SECTION 5: EXAMPLE

This is an example of the tax-related consequences of withdrawing dividends from your company.

We first look at what the company must pay in Corporation Tax (CT) to have net profits available to pay the dividend. We will then calculate the net amount that you will be left with as an individual after deduction of income tax.

We have used the following assumptions:

Total taxable profit made by the company	£70,000
Dividend withdrawn	£50,000
CT rate paid by the company	19%
Your highest personal tax rate on dividend	32.5%
Tax credit on the dividend	1/9

EXAMPLE 1.

COMPANY'S TAX POSITION		
	£	**%**
AFTER-TAX PROFITS NEEDED TO PAY THE DIVIDEND	50,000.00	100.00%
CT PAYABLE TO ARRIVE AT THESE PROFITS ((£50,000 / 81) x 19)	11,728.40	
THEREFORE THE COMPANY HAS TO MAKE PROFITS BEFORE TAX OF ((£50,000/ 81) x 100)	61,728.40	123.45%

YOUR TAX POSITION			
2005/06	**£**	**£**	**%**
DIVIDEND PAID	50,000.00	50,000.00	100.00%
TAX CREDIT ON DIVIDEND (1/9 x £50,000)	5,555.55		
GROSS TAXABLE DIVIDEND	55,555.55		
LESS TAX-FREE PERSONAL ALLOWANCE	-4,895.00		
TAXABLE DIVIDEND	50,660.55		
INCOME TAX AT 10% (ON £32,400)	-3,240.00		
INCOME TAX AT 32.5% (ON THE NEXT £18,260.55)	-5,934.68		
OFFSET TAX CREDIT ON DIVIDEND	5,555.55		
TOTAL TAXES PAID		-3,619.13	7.24%
NET DIVIDEND AVAILABLE TO SPEND		46,380.87	92.76%

EXAMPLE 2.

40% taxpayer. If your personal tax-free allowance of £4,895, 10% tax band and 22% tax band are already used elsewhere, the tax cost to you of taking a dividend as a higher rate taxpayer is as follows:

YOUR TAX POSITION			
2005/06	**£**	**£**	**%**
DIVIDEND PAID	50,000.00	50,000.00	100%
TAX CREDIT ON DIVIDEND *(1/9 x DIVIDEND PAID)*	5,555.55		
GROSS TAXABLE DIVIDEND *(DIVIDEND PLUS TAX CREDIT)*	55,555.55		
INCOME TAX AT 32.5%	-18,055.55		
TAX CREDIT SET AGAINST TAX ON DIVIDEND	5,555.55		
TOTAL TAXES		-12,500.00	25%
NET DIVIDEND AVAILABLE TO SPEND *(DIVIDEND PAID LESS TOTAL TAXES)*		37,500.00	75%

© PROFIT EXTRACTION, Indicator

SECTION 6: PROS & CONS

ADVANTAGES OF DIVIDENDS

1. No NI. There is no employers' or employees' NI due on the payment of a dividend.

2. No need to work. Non-working members of your family can receive income from the company in the form of dividends if they hold shares in the company (see Part 14).

3. More tax-efficient than bonus payments. If the company pays Corporation Tax (CT) at 19% or less it is more tax-efficient to pay profits out as a dividend rather than a bonus. If the company pays CT at 30% or the marginal rate of 32.75% it will pay more tax overall by retaining profits to pay out as a dividend rather than distributing a similar amount as a bonus.

4. Can be waived. A dividend can also be diverted from you to other shareholders if you waive your right to receive a particular dividend payment. To do this you must submit your waiver for the dividend to the company before the shareholders approve the directors' recommendation. You cannot waive the dividend after you obtain the right to receive the dividend.

5. No further tax to pay. If your total income is less than £37,295 (£4,895 + £32,400) for the tax year 2005/06, you will have no further tax to pay on dividends you receive.

DISADVANTAGES OF DIVIDENDS

1. Non-refundable tax credit. If the tax credit attached to the net dividend is not used to offset the tax due, it cannot be repaid.

2. Cannot be used as the basis of pension contributions. Dividends are not earned income so the dividends received must be ignored when calculating the maximum that can be paid into a pension scheme.

3. Cannot deduct expenses. Deducting expenses cannot reduce the amount of dividend that is taxable in your hands.

4. May increase share value. Regular dividends paid at a high level can increase the value of small shareholdings in the company. The value of large shareholdings will normally be based on the value of the assets less the liabilities the company holds. The value of smaller shareholdings will depend on the pattern of dividends the shareholders expect to receive.

5. Illegal dividend. If a dividend is paid when the company's accounts show that there was insufficient profit retained after tax to cover that dividend, the payment will be illegal under company law. An illegal dividend should be repaid. If it's not, the Taxman may argue that the payment was a loan to the shareholders.

6. Must be paid to all shareholders. The shareholders of one class of shares must all receive the same amount of dividend per share, although individual shareholders may waive their right to an entire dividend payment (see Part 14).

DIVIDENDS

Profit Extraction

Interest

SECTION 1: METHOD

WHAT IS INTEREST?

When the company borrows from a bank it must pay interest on the money advanced. If you have a director's loan account with the company that's in credit, i.e. the company is holding money that is due to you, you are also effectively lending money to it. You can ask the company to pay you interest on the credit balance of your director's loan account, and on any other funds you have lent to it.

HOW DO YOU CHARGE INTEREST?

The interest can be paid by cheque or by electronic transfer to your personal bank account or credited to your director's loan account (thereby increasing the balance owed by the company to you). The payment can be made on a regular basis, either monthly or quarterly, or annually if you wish. However, as the company has to tell the Taxman how much interest it has paid to you each quarter, maybe it's convenient for it to pay the interest due to you on the same basis.

Interest certificate. In order to help you with your tax affairs the company should issue you with an annual certificate of interest (see Appendix 2) for the relevant tax year.

WHAT RATE CAN YOU USE?

The company should pay a commercial rate of interest on the money it has borrowed from you. This may be 5% or 6% over the bank base rate. However, if the company pays more than a commercial rate, the Taxman may view the excess as a payment of salary and require the company to deduct income tax and NI from it.

© PROFIT EXTRACTION, Indicator

SECTION 2: YOUR COMPANY

IS INTEREST PAID TAX-DEDUCTIBLE FOR THE COMPANY?

Yes. The company can deduct the interest paid to you from its profits before the calculation of Corporation Tax.

DOES THE COMPANY DEDUCT TAX FROM YOUR INTEREST?

Yes. Generally a company must deduct income tax at the rate of 20% from interest paid to you as an individual. This 20% must be reported and paid over to the Taxman using Form CT61. This form needs to be completed and submitted to the Taxman within 14 days of the last day of the quarters that end on: March 31, June 30, September 30 and December 31. So if the company pays interest in those quarters it has some administration to do.

No. The company does not have to deduct income tax from the interest paid to you in the following circumstances: (1) you provide the funds to the company for a defined period which is less than a year; (2) the loan to the company cannot be extended beyond a year; and (3) the interest due is calculated on a daily or monthly basis and is not expressed in terms of an annual rate.

Taxman's view. If all three conditions above apply the interest is called "short interest" and the company does not have to deduct income tax from it. However, the Taxman will try and argue that almost all interest paid to a director of the company is not "short interest" as the loan will always be capable of extending beyond a year, even if the money was repaid within twelve months.

WHAT IS THE NI COST?

None. There is no employers' NI payable on interest paid to you.

DOES IT MATTER HOW MUCH INTEREST IS PAID?

Commercial rate. If the interest is paid at a rate that is higher than a commercial rate the Taxman will treat it as if it were salary and ask the company to pay income tax and NI on the excess. Remember, a commercial interest rate may be 5% or 6% over the bank base rate.

Small profits. If the interest paid reduces the company's profits below £10,000 for the year, the company will get no effective tax relief for that interest payment as profits below that level are taxed at 0% (if no dividends are paid). So reconsider your "final" interest payment when finalising the company's annual accounts.

INTEREST

SECTION 3: YOU

SHOULD INTEREST BE SHOWN ON YOUR TAX RETURN?

Yes. The interest you receive from the company must be shown on your tax return, under "Income from UK savings and investments". You should copy the amount of net interest paid from the certificate (see Appendix 2) provided by the company, to your tax return. You are also required to enter the amount of tax deducted and the gross amount of interest paid before tax.

WHAT IS THE NI COST?

None. There is no employees' NI due on interest paid to you by the company, as long as the rate used is not in excess of a commercial one.

CAN YOU DEDUCT ANY EXPENSES FROM THIS INTEREST?

Possibly. If you have borrowed from a bank to lend money to the company the interest you're charged by the lender can be deducted as an expense on your tax return, but only if the following conditions apply: (1) the company must be a close company which means it is controlled by its directors or there are five or fewer shareholders; (2) the company must either be trading or control a company that is trading, or it must hold land that is let to someone connected with the company; and (3) you must own at least 5% of the company's shares or be able to control at least 5% of the shares through your relatives or associates at the time the interest is paid.

AT WHAT RATE WILL INTEREST FINALLY BE TAXED?

It depends. The tax you pay on interest received from the company will depend on the level of your other income in the same tax year. The interest is taxed after taking account of salary/bonuses but before adding dividends to your total income. If the company has already deducted income tax at 20% you do not have to pay any further tax as a basic rate (22%) taxpayer. If you pay tax at the higher rate of 40% you will have to pay further income tax at the rate of 20% on the interest received.

INTEREST

© PROFIT EXTRACTION, Indicator

SECTION 4: VAT

ARE THERE ANY CONSEQUENCES FOR VAT?

None. There are no VAT consequences of receiving interest from the company.

SECTION 5: EXAMPLE

This is an example of the tax-related consequences of withdrawing interest from your company.

We first look at what the payment of interest costs your company in net terms. We are taking into account the fact that the interest is tax-deductible for the company. We will then calculate the net amount that you will be left with as an individual.

We have used the following assumptions:

Loan made by you to the company	£50,000
Rate of interest charged on that loan (base plus 6%)	10%
Interest paid for the year	£5,000
Corporation Tax (CT) rate paid by company	19%
Income tax deducted by the company	20%
Your highest personal tax rate	40%

COMPANY'S TAX POSITION			
	£	£	CT PAYABLE
TAXABLE PROFIT IN COMPANY BEFORE DEDUCTION OF INTEREST PAID TO YOU		70,000.00	13,300.00
GROSS INTEREST PAID	5,000.00	-5,000.00	
NET PROFIT AFTER INTEREST		65,000.00	12,350.00
CT SAVED BY PAYING INTEREST	-950.00		-950.00
NET COST TO THE COMPANY (COST LESS CT SAVED)	4,050.00		

NET COST AS A PERCENTAGE OF THE GROSS INTEREST	81%

YOUR TAX POSITION			
GROSS INTEREST		5,000.00	100%
INCOME TAX AT 40% (ON £5,000)	-2,000.00		
TOTAL TAXES PAID*		-2,000.00	40%
NET INTEREST AVAILABLE TO SPEND		3,000.00	60%

*£1,000 (£5,000 x 20%) of this bill has already been paid to the Taxman by the company, after it was deducted from your interest payments.

© PROFIT EXTRACTION, Indicator

INTEREST

SECTION 6: PROS AND CONS

ADVANTAGES OF INTEREST

1. No NI. There is no NI due on the interest paid to you by the company.

2. Commercial rate. You can charge the company a commercial interest rate on the funds it holds on your behalf, or the money you lend to it. That interest rate will be higher than the rate you would receive from a bank or building society if you deposited the same funds with those institutions.

3. Flexible rate. The rate of interest paid by the company is totally flexible. It can be set at any rate you please as long as it does not exceed the commercial rate that the company would pay if it borrowed the same funds from an external source.

4. Reduces Corporation Tax. The company can deduct the interest it pays you from its profits before Corporation Tax is payable.

5. Tax-free capital. You can withdraw the capital from the company on which the interest is paid at any time, with no tax consequences.

DISADVANTAGES OF INTEREST

1. Capital required. You must lend the company money for it to be able to pay you interest on that capital. Alternatively you can leave taxed earnings or dividends within the company in your director's loan account, and ask the company to pay interest on those retained funds.

2. Excessive rate. If the interest is paid at a rate in excess of a reasonable commercial one the Taxman will demand that income tax and NI be deducted by the company from the excess.

3. Loan is unsecured. The money you lend to the company is at risk and may not be returned if the company gets into financial difficulties. This concern can, however, be used to justify a higher rate of interest.

4. Not earnings for a pension. You cannot use your interest income to increase the maximum pension contribution you can pay.

5. No State benefits. As the interest does not attract NI, the interest you receive does not allow you to qualify for State Social Security benefits or a State Pension.

6. Tax deducted. The company must deduct income tax at 20% from the interest paid to you, unless that interest is so-called "short interest".

INTEREST

Profit Extraction

Rent

SECTION 1: METHOD

WHAT DO WE MEAN BY RENT?

Rent is a sum you receive from the company in return for allowing it to use property you own. The property may be a commercial or a domestic building, land, even part of a building. On a smaller scale, even if your company uses the garage attached to your home to e.g. to store stock, you can let it out and receive rent in return.

HOW SHOULD YOU WITHDRAW RENT?

Agreement. The rent should normally be paid under a formal lease agreement between you and the company. This lease agreement will stipulate how often the rent should be paid, either monthly, quarterly or annually. The company should pay the rent by giving you a cheque for the amount due or by making an electronic transfer to your private bank account.

Minutes. If, as a private individual, you enter into such a contract with your company, you should tell all the other directors at a board meeting. The minutes of the meeting should record when the lease agreement is due to start and how much will be paid under it.

Share it. If the property is jointly owned, say by you and your spouse, the rent should be paid to you both. Alternatively you can receive all the rent on behalf of the other owner or owners and pay out the proportion which is due to them.

Leave it in the company. You can leave the rent due to you in your director's current account. This can help the company with its cash flow, and the delayed withdrawal has no tax consequences for you or your company.

IS IT IMPORTANT HOW MUCH RENT YOU CHARGE?

Yes. You can charge the company as little rent as you wish for using your property. However, if the rent is not enough to cover the expenses connected with the property, such as repairs and insurance, you will lose money. Any loss you make from letting property can only be set against profits from letting in the future; it cannot be used to reduce tax due on your other income in the same year or earlier years.

Disclosure. If the lease is for a significant sum compared to the other expenses of the company, the amount paid will have to be shown in the notes to your company's annual accounts.

RENT

© PROFIT EXTRACTION, Indicator

SECTION 2: YOUR COMPANY

IS RENT PAID TAX-DEDUCTIBLE FOR THE COMPANY?

Yes. As long as the property is used by the company for its business it can deduct the full cost of the rent paid from its profits. The company may use the property for its business and it may even have occasion to use a domestic property to provide living accommodation for its employees. This is still regarded as business use because the employee who occupies the flat or house is taxed on the rental value.

WHAT IS THE NI COST?

None. There is no employers' NI on rent paid to you.

SHOULD THE COMPANY DEDUCT ANY TAXES FROM THE RENT?

No. Rent is not earnings so it should not be taxed under the Pay-As-You-Earn (PAYE) system.

Overseas. If you live outside the UK and let a property here for more than £100 per week, income tax should be deducted from the rent before the residue is paid to you. The company must deduct tax at 22% of the gross rent and pay it over to the Taxman each quarter. You can, however, apply to the Taxman for the rent to be paid to you without deduction of tax.

DOES IT MATTER HOW MUCH RENT IS PAID?

Yes. If the company pays you a very high rent (above the market rate), the Taxman may argue that the excess is actually a disguised form of salary. He will insist that any excess is taxed like a salary (see Part 1), and will require the company to deduct tax under PAYE.

Corporation Tax. The rent paid by the company will reduce its profits and the amount of Corporation Tax (CT) it has to pay. The rates of CT payable depend on the level of profits after deduction of expenses such as rent. However, you need to ensure that the rent is not taxed at a higher rate in your hands than the profits would be taxed at if they remained in the company.

Example.

> The company may save CT at, say, 19% by paying you rent which you have to
> pay tax on at your highest rate of 40%. This simple comparison does not take
> into account the expenses that you could set against the rent.

Flexibility. If the company suffers a bad trading period you can reduce the rent due on the property to help its cash flow.

RENT

SECTION 3: YOU

SHOULD THE RENT BE SHOWN ON YOUR TAX RETURN?

Yes. The rent you receive from the company is income from land or property. If the property is in the UK you should include the rent on "Land and Property" supplementary pages with your tax return. If the property is abroad (e.g. a villa in Spain) you should fill in details of the rents received and expenses set against those rents on the "Foreign Income" supplementary pages.

If you have not received a tax return, or a notice reminding you to complete it electronically, you must ask the Taxman to set a record up for you on his self-assessment system. If you receive rent for the first time and do not normally complete a tax return, you must tell him by October 5 after the end of the tax year when you started to receive the rent.

Rent-a-room relief. Letting a room in your own home is normally tax-free if the total rent received in a tax year is less than £4,250. Unfortunately, this tax relief does not apply if the room is used by a business for an office or for storage. However, if the room is used by the company to provide accommodation to an employee, the rent-a-room relief does apply.

Jointly owned. If the property is owned with another person, you should only report the portion of the rent and expenses on your tax return that relates to your share. However, if you own the property jointly with your spouse you normally have to share the income equally, whatever your actual share in the property. If you declare your actual ownership in the property you can divide the rent and expenses along those lines.

Example.

You contributed £10,000 to buy a property whilst your spouse paid £40,000. The property is let to your company for £5,000 per year and there are £1,000 of expenses relating to the letting. You and your spouse should each show rents received of £2,500 on your respective tax returns and expenses of £500, even if all the rent is paid to you and you meet all the costs.

If you both sign an election telling the Taxman the actual percentage of the property you each own, you can split the rent with £1,000 shown on your tax return and £4,000 on your spouse's. The expenses should be divided in the same way.

WHAT IS THE NI COST?

None. Rent is not earnings under the NI rules, so employees' NI is not due on rent paid to you.

CAN YOU DEDUCT ANY EXPENSES FROM THE RENT?

Yes. You can deduct any expenses from the rent which are wholly and exclusively connected with the land or building that is let. These expenses may include:

• interest paid on a loan used to buy or improve the property

- repairs to the building (but not the cost of improvements)

- cost of services such as water rates (if the tenant does not pay them directly)

- legal costs of drawing up a short-term lease

- buildings insurance

- industrial buildings allowances

- capital allowances on any plant or equipment fixed to the building

- security guards to protect the property (if you pay for these yourself)

- accountancy fees for working out your profit after deductions.

Proportion. If you let part of a building to the company, but pay all the main services, you should set a proportion of those costs against the rent received.

Example.

> *You occupy the upper two floors of a three-storey property, while your company trades from the ground floor. The total cost of the mortgage interest, buildings insurance, heating and lighting should be apportioned so that one third is deducted as an expense from the rent the company pays to you.*

> *You may feel that the company is responsible for more than one third of the total electricity bill, because it uses powerful lighting or industrial air heaters in the retail space on the ground floor. If this is the case you should split the costs on a reasonable basis and make a note of how you reached that apportionment in case the Taxman ever asks you to justify your calculations.*

Business rates. The local authority can charge business rates for any property or part of a property that is used by a business. Council Tax is paid for domestic properties. If you let part of your home to your company you can charge part of the Council Tax you pay for the whole property as an expense against the rent. However, if the local authority decides to inspect your home and finds that it is used for business they may reduce your Council Tax and charge business rates on the part of the property that is let to the company. The company will be due to pay the business rates as it is the legal occupier of that part of your home under the lease agreement.

AT WHAT RATE WILL THE RENT FINALLY BE TAXED?

The rate of income tax that applies to the rent less expenses depends on your total income during the tax year.

SHOULD ANY TAX BE PAID IN ADVANCE ON THE RENT?

No. Unless you are normally resident overseas the company should not deduct tax from the rent it pays you.

RENT

SECTION 4: VAT

WHEN DO YOU CHARGE VAT ON RENTS?

Not registered for VAT. You don't charge VAT on top of the rent you charge the company. However, you might end up with some irrecoverable input VAT suffered on the cost of acquiring the building originally and/or refurbishing it. The rule is no VAT charge, no VAT recovery!

Registered for VAT. Providing the building is used for commercial purposes (not a residential property), you can register for VAT and opt to tax it, which means charging VAT on the rent. However, you are now able recover all the VAT on your costs. Of course this means completing a VAT return and paying any VAT you owe.

Once registered for VAT and having opted to tax the building, you will have to charge VAT on any service charges you bill the company for.

CAN THE COMPANY RECOVER THE VAT?

Provided your company does not make exempt supplies it can recover the VAT on the rent if you charge it.

WHAT'S THE BEST THING TO DO?

Scenario 1. If you've been charged substantial VAT on acquiring the building or incur significant input VAT on expenditure to the building (e.g. during a refurbishment), then register for VAT and opt to tax and recover the VAT now. If the company is able to recover the VAT that you charge it then there's no loss to anybody, the VAT just moves round in a circle but you have also recovered the VAT that you incurred.

Scenario 2. The same situation as above but the company cannot recover some or all of the VAT that it is charged. Over time you will hand back the VAT you have recovered as output tax on the rents, but this can take a long time. Meanwhile a significant cash flow advantage is achieved.

Scenario 3. If your VAT costs are small don't bother to opt to tax. There is no cash flow advantage in this situation.

© PROFIT EXTRACTION, Indicator

SECTION 5: EXAMPLE

This is an example of the tax-related consequences of extracting rent from your company.

We first look at what payment of the rent costs your company in net terms. We are taking into account the fact that the rent is tax-deductible for the company. We will then calculate the net amount that you will be left with as an individual after deduction of income tax.

We have used the following assumptions:

Rent	£15,000
Corporation Tax (CT) rate paid by company	19%
Your highest personal tax rate	40%

COMPANY'S TAX POSITION			
	£	£	CT PAYABLE
TAXABLE PROFIT IN THE COMPANY BEFORE DEDUCTION OF RENT PAID TO YOU		70,000.00	13,300.00
GROSS RENT PAID	15,000.00		
TOTAL COSTS		-15,000.00	
NET PROFIT AFTER RENT		55,000.00	10,450.00
CT SAVED BY PAYING RENT	-2,850.00		-2,850.00
NET COST TO THE COMPANY (COSTS LESS CT SAVED)	12,150.00		

NET COST AS A PERCENTAGE OF RENT PAID	81%

YOUR TAX POSITION			
RENT DUE TO YOU		15,000.00	100%
INCOME TAX AT 40% (ON £15,000 IF THERE ARE NO EXPENSES TO DEDUCT FROM IT)	-6,000.00		
TOTAL TAXES PAID		-6,000.00	40%
NET RENT AVAILABLE TO SPEND		9,000.00	60%

SECTION 6: PROS AND CONS

ADVANTAGES OF RENT

1. Reduces Corporation Tax. By paying you rent, the company reduces its taxable profits which in turn reduces the Corporation Tax (CT) it pays. If the company's profits are reduced to £10,000 or less for the year it pays no CT at all (unless it pays a dividend).

2. No NI. There is no employers' or employees' NI to pay on rents.

3. Expenses. You can deduct a wide range of expenses from the rent you receive before it is taxed, as long as they relate to the property.

4. Diversion. If the property is owned jointly with your spouse, 50% of the income can be taxed in their name at their own tax rate.

5. Business asset taper relief. If you let your property to a trading company, it is treated as a business asset for Capital Gains Tax while that company uses it. When you sell the property, the period that it was a business asset will help to reduce the Capital Gains Tax you pay on any profit. The maximum taper relief discount you can get is 75% of your gain, and this as quickly as two years after you acquire the property. This is a complex area, so we suggest you seek specialist advice.

DISADVANTAGES OF RENT

1. Property required. You need to own or lease land or buildings as a private person in order to let that property to the company, so in most cases to be able to charge rent there is a capital investment to be made first.

2. Restricted to market rent. Any rent paid to you that is in excess of the market rate for the property, may be taxed as additional salary.

3. Not earnings. The rent you receive is ignored in the calculation of the maximum pension contributions you can pay.

4. No State benefits. The rent you receive will not entitle you to claim State benefits if you become unemployed, sick or are bereaved. Rents do not give you any entitlement to a State Pension.

5. Business rates. If you let part of your own home to the company to use as an office or for storage, the local authority may seek to charge business rates instead of Council Tax on that part. Business rates are normally higher than Council Tax.

RENT

© PROFIT EXTRACTION, indicator

Profit Extraction

Loans

SECTION 1: METHOD

WHAT IS A LOAN?

A loan from the company to you can take many forms. It may be a formal arrangement under which the company provides you with funds which you agree to repay by a certain date, possibly with interest. Or it can be a payment in advance of e.g. a dividend that's paid to you by the company in the future.

Helping hand. If the company puts down a deposit to help you buy a house or a car, the money provided can either be treated as a bonus or as a loan. If treated as a bonus, you will be taxed on the full amount paid by the company. However, if the deposit paid is treated as a loan to you by the company you are not taxed on the amount of the advance, but you may be taxed on an official rate of interest (currently 5% p.a.) for the loan.

HOW DO YOU TAKE OUT A LOAN?

You can withdraw the loan in the form of a cheque, cash, or transfer to your private bank account. However, the money paid needs to be accurately recorded as a loan in the company's accounts. The best way to do this is to have a separate account shown in the company's books as a director's loan account. This should record all the amounts paid to you as loans and the dates and values of any repayments you make.

Paperwork. You do not normally have to sign a loan agreement when you borrow money from your company. However, if you are not the only shareholder, company law states that you should get the written permission of the other shareholders before you can borrow more than £5,000.

Overdrawn. You can withdraw money by cheque or cash payments, or the company may buy things for you and add the cost of these items to your director's current account. If a close check is not kept on this account, you might draw more money out of the company than is due to you, so the account becomes overdrawn. This is treated as a loan while it's overdrawn.

WHAT IS THE MAXIMUM LOAN YOU CAN HAVE?

Unrestricted. In principle you can withdraw as much as you want as a loan. If you pay a reasonable level of interest to the company on the sum borrowed, you will not be taxed on the loan.

For tax. However, if you borrow more than £5,000 and pay only a very low rate of interest, or no interest at all, the Taxman says you have received a benefit-in-kind of an interest-free loan, and will charge you tax on that benefit. The company may also have to pay a tax charge if the loan has not been repaid by nine months after the year in which you first received the loan.

© PROFIT EXTRACTION, Indicator

SECTION 2: YOUR COMPANY

IS A LOAN TAX-DEDUCTIBLE FOR THE COMPANY?

No. The company cannot deduct the capital advanced to you as a loan from its profits. The loan is treated as coming out of the company's capital reserves. Any expenses the company incurs in connection with making the loan to you cannot be deducted from profits.

DOES THE COMPANY DEDUCT ANY TAX FROM THE LOAN?

No. The loan is not classed as earnings, so it should not have tax or NI deducted under the Pay-As-You Earn system.

Close company. A close company has to pay an additional tax charge amounting to 25% of the loan, the so-called Section 419 charge, if it makes a loan to one of its directors or shareholders and that loan is not repaid in full by nine months after the end of the accounting period during which the money was first provided. A close company is one that is controlled by its directors who are also the shareholders, or one that has five or fewer shareholders. The Section 419 tax charge is refunded by the Taxman nine months after the end of the accounting period in which the loan is repaid.

Example.

> The company makes a loan of £10,000 to a director on January 1, 2005, which is reported in the company's Corporation Tax return for the year ended December 31, 2005. The company pays a Section 419 tax charge of £2,500 (£10,000 x 25%) on October 1, 2006 as the loan is still outstanding on that date. The loan is repaid in full to the company on November 30, 2006 and this is reported in the company's return for the year ended December 31, 2006. The Taxman repays the Section 419 tax charge by offsetting the £2,500 against Corporation Tax due for payment on October 1, 2007.

You only pay once. Even if the loan remains outstanding for more than one accounting period the Section 419 tax charge is only paid once.

> In the example above the loan is outstanding for the whole of the year 2005 and most of 2006, but the Section 419 tax charge is only levied once on October 1, 2006. If the loan is not repaid until October 31, 2008 there would be no further tax charged but the original Section 419 tax would not be refunded to the company until October 1, 2009.

Small loans included. Any size of advance or loan can trigger a Section 419 charge. All loans are added together.

Written off. If the loan to you is released, written off or forgiven by the company, so that you are not required to repay the money, the Section 419 tax charge is refunded as if the loan had been repaid on the date it was written off. However, you will be taxed as if you had received a bonus of an amount equal to the loan written off, on the date that loan was forgiven.

LOANS

DOES IT MATTER HOW BIG THE LOAN IS?

Yes. Technically it's illegal for a company to lend more than £5,000 to one of its directors unless the shareholders have approved the loan and the money is to be used to help the individual perform his duties as a director of the company. If you want to borrow more than £5,000 from your company you should tell all the shareholders how much you need, what the money is to be used for, and get their written approval. This procedure is to protect the funds the other shareholders have invested in the company from being siphoned off by one director. If you are the only shareholder and director of the company this obviously does not apply.

Disclosure. Even if you are the only shareholder and director of the company, the annual accounts must show the value of loans outstanding to the directors and their immediate families. This disclosure is required to inform the other people and organisations who are owed money by the company, how their cash is being used. If a bank manager can see the funds he lent to the company have been provided to the directors for their own private purposes, he may not be very happy. The bank may have the power under its loan agreement to demand an immediate repayment, possibly from the directors personally.

WHAT IS THE NI COST?

Employers' NI. If the company lends more than £5,000 to an employee or director on favourable terms so that the borrower pays very little or no interest, the borrower has received a taxable benefit. The company must show the cash equivalent value of this benefit on the annual Form P11D (Return of Expenses and Benefits). The company must also pay employers' NI on the cash equivalent value of the benefit by July 6 after the end of the tax year during which the loan exceeded £5,000.

Cash equivalent. The cash equivalent value of the benefit of the loan is the interest that would have been payable if you had paid interest at the official rate (less any actual interest paid by you).

Example.

> If you had borrowed £10,000 from your company on April 6, 2005 and then repaid the full amount by April 5, 2006, with an official interest rate of 5%, the taxable benefit and NI due is:

TAXABLE BENEFIT	£10,000 x 5%	£500
EMPLOYERS' NI	£500 x 12.8%	£64

Variable loan. There are two ways of calculating the cash equivalent value, the "averaging method", which is normally used and the "exact daily method". The two methods will produce the same result if the level of the loan does not vary during the tax year. However, in the real world, a director will often repay a loan gradually or increase his borrowing during the year.

Example.

> You borrow £8,000 on April 6, 2005 and repay £3,000 on February 5, 2006 leaving a balance of £5,000 still outstanding on April 5, 2006. The cash equivalent value of the benefit and the employers' NI due calculated using the two methods are:

AVERAGING METHOD		£
AVERAGE BALANCE	(£8,000+£5,000) / 2	6,500.00
TAXABLE BENEFIT	£6,500 x 5%	325.00
EMPLOYERS' NI	£325 x 12.8%	41.60

EXACT DAILY METHOD		£
306 DAYS TO FEBRUARY 5, 2006	£8,000 x 5% x 306/365	335.34
59 DAYS TO APRIL 5, 2006	£5,000 x 5% x 59/365	40.41
TOTAL CASH EQUIVALENT:		375.75
EMPLOYERS' NI	£375.75 x 12.8%	48.10

In this case, the "exact daily method" produces a higher taxable benefit and a higher level of employers' NI due, but it sometimes produces a lower figure. You should normally use the "averaging method", but keep a check on the result of the exact method calculation.

Taxman's choice. Where the loan balance was much higher earlier in the tax year than at the end, the exact method will produce a much higher figure of benefit and NI due than the averaging method. In this case the Taxman may insist that the exact method is used. The company must show the highest balance of the loan on Form P11D.

SECTION 3: YOU

WHAT DO YOU PUT ON YOUR TAX RETURN?

You do not have show a company loan on your tax return. If you borrow less than £5,000 there are no tax consequences for you. Also, if the company is in the business of providing commercial loans and your loan is provided on similar commercial terms, you will not be taxed on it.

Interest. If you borrow more than £5,000 and pay less than the official interest rate (currently 5%) on the outstanding balance you have received a benefit-in-kind. The cash equivalent value of the benefit should be calculated by the company and shown on Form P11D which it prepares each year. The company must provide you with a copy of the information shown on the P11D by July 6 each year. You need to copy the details of taxable benefits shown on the "Employment" pages of your tax return in the section titled "Benefits and expenses".

WHAT IS THE NI COST?

None. You do not have to pay NI on the money you borrow from the company.

CAN YOU DEDUCT ANY EXPENSES FROM THE BENEFIT OF A LOAN?

No. The loan is not taxable whilst it is still repayable to the company. If the loan is written off, or forgiven, so you do not have to pay it back, you will be taxed on the sum advanced as if it were a bonus. In that case there are a very limited number of expenses that you can deduct from the amount provided as a loan (see Part 1).

AT WHAT RATE WILL A LOAN FINALLY BE TAXED?

You do not have to pay tax on the loan from the company, but the cash equivalent value of the benefit of a low-interest loan will be taxed if the amount borrowed is more than £5,000. The rate of tax that applies to your earnings depends on your total taxable income during the tax year.

IS ANY TAX DUE IN ADVANCE?

No. There is no tax to pay on the loan, so no tax should be paid in advance.

© PROFIT EXTRACTION, Indicator

LOANS

SECTION 4: VAT

ARE THERE ANY CONSEQUENCES FOR VAT?

None. Drawing a loan from your company has no VAT consequences at all. Loans made available to employees and directors are not subject to VAT so no VAT invoice should be issued when the loan is drawn or repaid.

SECTION 5: EXAMPLE

This is an example of the tax related consequences of withdrawing a loan from your company as we have discussed on the previous pages.

We have used the following assumptions:

Company year-end	March 31, 2006
Loan capital withdrawn on April 6, 2005	£50,000
Loan capital repaid April 5, 2006	£50,000
Interest charged on the loan	0%
Official interest rate on benefit of interest-free loan	5%
Employers' NI paid on benefit of interest-free loan	12.8%
Highest personal tax rate	40%
Corporation Tax (CT) rate paid by company on its profits	19%

The benefit-in-kind is therefore £50,000 x 5% (the official rate of interest), which is £2,500.

We have also assumed that the company has the necessary cash reserved to lend you the money without having to increase its own borrowings.

COMPANY'S TAX POSITION		£	CT PAYABLE
PROFITS MADE BY THE COMPANY		70,000.00	13,300.00
EMPLOYERS' NI ON BENEFIT-IN-KIND *(12.8% ON £2,500)*	320.00	-320.00	
TAXABLE PROFITS		69,680.00	13,239.20
CT SAVED BY PROVIDING A LOAN	-60.80		-60.80
NET COST FOR THE COMPANY *(LOAN COSTS LESS CT SAVING)*	259.20		

NET COST AS A PERCENTAGE OF THE LOAN	0.5%

YOUR TAX POSITION			
TAX YEAR ENDED APRIL 5, 2006	£	£	%
LOAN WITHDRAWN		50,000.00	100%
CASH EQUIVALENT OF THE INTEREST BENEFIT-IN-KIND *(£50,000 x 5%)*	2,500.00		
TOTAL ANNUAL TAXES PAID *(£2,500 x 40%)*		-1,000.00	2%
NET LOAN AVAILABLE *(BUT IT MUST BE REPAID)*		49,000.00	98%

However, the loan must be repaid eventually, so you could end up taking a dividend or bonus to clear the loan, with their respective after-tax costs.

LOANS

© PROFIT EXTRACTION, Indicator

SECTION 6: PROS & CONS

ADVANTAGES OF A LOAN:

1. Tax and NI-free. You can borrow up to £5,000 from your company without being taxed personally. There is also no NI to pay on the loan while the capital borrowed is repayable.

2. Up to 21 months. If you borrow from your company at the beginning of its accounting year, the capital can remain outstanding for up to 21 months (the company year plus nine months) with no tax charge being applied.

3. Easy application. There are no formal loan approval procedures or application forms to complete when you borrow from your company.

4. Low interest. You can pay either a very low rate of interest or no interest at all on a loan from your company. If you pay at least the official rate of interest of 5%, you can borrow without restriction at very favourable rates.

5. Can be diverted. Your company can advance a small loan to a member of your family without you being taxed on it.

DISADVANTAGES OF A LOAN:

1. Needs to be repaid. The loan capital must be repaid to the company at some point. If the loan is forgiven you will be taxed on the capital sum as if you had received a bonus payment of that amount on the date the loan was forgiven.

2. Tax charge. If the loan is still outstanding nine months after the end of the accounting year during which it was provided, the company must pay a tax charge of 25% for the capital advanced, however big or small the amount of the loan. However, this is refundable after the loan has been cleared.

3. Tax on cash equivalent value. For a loan in excess of £5,000 you will be taxed on the cash value of the benefit of receiving a low-interest loan. Currently this is 5% of the loan balance, at your top rate of income tax.

4. Employers' NI. The company must pay employers' NI on the cash equivalent value of the benefit of providing you with a low-interest loan.

5. Shareholder approval. If the loan is for more than £5,000 written approval should be obtained from all the company shareholders.

6. Accounts disclosure. The company's annual accounts must disclose the nature and amounts of loans provided to the directors.

LOANS

Profit Extraction

Company cars

SECTION 1: METHOD

WHAT IS MEANT BY A COMPANY CAR?

When your company buys or leases a car directly and allows you to drive it, it's known as a company car.

HOW SHOULD THE COMPANY CAR BE PROVIDED?

Your company. The car should be owned or leased by the company and lent to you to use as you wish. The company should insure the vehicle for both business and pleasure use, and pay for the car tax, all repair and servicing costs. You should not take on the ownership of the car, although you can be its registered keeper.

You. If you sign a lease agreement in your name for a car, but the company pays the instalments on your behalf, it's not a company car. In this case you are financially responsible for the car as the lease is in your name.

DOES IT MATTER WHAT TYPE OF CAR YOU HAVE?

Emissions. You are taxed on the so-called cash equivalent of the benefit of having a company car. The cash equivalent is calculated as a percentage of the car's list price for every year or part of a year in which you can use it. The percentage of the list price used depends on the official CO_2 emissions figure for the car, which is fixed at the time of manufacture and is shown on the vehicle's registration document (V5) for cars registered since March 1, 2001. For older cars you can check the CO_2 emissions figure on the Vehicle Certification Agency's website: http://www.vcacarfueldata.org.uk/.

List price. We have referred to the list price of the car rather than its cost. This is deliberate because the cash equivalent for the car is calculated according to its list price, not what the company actually paid for it. The list price is the price that a single car would have been sold at in the UK on the day before it was first registered. This price does not include any discounts given by a dealer, but it should include the cost of any extras worth over £100 that are added at any time. The list price of cars can generally be checked on the manufacturer's website.

© PROFIT EXTRACTION, Indicator

COMPANY CARS

SECTION 2: YOUR COMPANY

IS THE COST OF THE CAR TAX-DEDUCTIBLE?

Yes. The cost of providing the car is tax-deductible for the company, but its full purchase price cannot be deducted from the company's profits in one year. When the company buys a car, the most it can normally deduct in one year is 25% of the cost (up to a maximum of £3,000).

Example.

The company pays £20,000 for a car, so the tax deduction for the first four years is:

	YEAR 1	YEAR 2	YEAR 3	YEAR 4
TAX DEDUCTION	*£3,000*	*£3,000*	*£3,000*	*£2,750*
TAX VALUE AT THE END OF THE YEAR	*£17,000*	*£14,000*	*£11,000*	*£8,250*

Loan interest. If the company takes out a loan to buy the car it can claim a tax deduction for the interest paid on the loan plus any administration fee it pays to the lender. It will also be able to deduct the acquisition cost of the car spread over a number of years as shown in the example above.

Leasing restriction. By a lease we mean a contract hire agreement under which the company pays an initial sum and then monthly payments for a set period. The car is returned to the leasing company at the end of the agreement. Although the company may pay out more at the start of the lease it must spread the cost evenly for tax purposes over the full period of the lease. Indeed, if the retail price of the car is more than £12,000 the tax deduction for leasing costs is restricted by the amount by which the car's retail price exceeds £12,000.

Example.

The company leases a car that has a retail price of £20,000, over a three-year term. This is £8,000 more than the price limit of £12,000, or 40% of the retail price. So half of this excess i.e. 20% of the leasing costs, cannot be claimed as a tax deduction. The company pays £4,000 as an initial payment plus 36 monthly payments of £250 (total cost: £13,000). The leasing payments and the amounts that are tax-deductible for the company are as follows:

	YEAR 1	YEAR2	YEAR 3	TOTAL
PAYMENTS	*£7,000*	*£3,000*	*£3,000*	*£13,000*
SPREAD EVENLY	*£4,333*	*£4,333*	*£4,334*	*£13,000*
LESS 20%	*-£867*	*-£867*	*-£866*	*£2,600*
TAX DEDUCTION	*£3,466*	*£3,466*	*£3,468*	*£10,400*

Low-emission cars. If the company purchases a new car with an official CO_2 emissions figure of 120gr/km or less, it can deduct the full cost of the car in the year of purchase. This applies for new cars

© PROFIT EXTRACTION, Indicator

COMPANY CARS

purchased between April 16, 2002 and April 1, 2008. If the company prefers to lease such a car the tax deduction for the leasing cost is not restricted for this type of car (see Leasing restriction above).

WHAT IS THE NI COST?

Employers' NI. The company must pay NI on the cash equivalent of the company car. This NI is paid annually by July 6 following the end of the tax year during which the car was provided.

Company car benefit. The company has to calculate the cash equivalent value of your company car in order to complete your Form P11D. This is the same figure that it will have to pay employers' NI on. How does it calculate the cash equivalent value? It's the list price of the car multiplied by the taxable benefit percentage. If you know the CO_2 emissions rating of the car you can look up the benefit percentage in the appendix to the Taxman's leaflet IR172 Income Tax and Company Cars. This is available from the Employers' Orderline on 0845 7646646 or can be viewed on the Taxman's website at http://www.hmrc.gov.uk/pdfs/ir172.htm.

Example.

> Say you choose a petrol car with a list price of £20,000 and a CO_2 emissions rating of 210 gr/km. For 2005/06 the benefit percentage for this car, according to the Taxman's leaflet, is 29%. Therefore, the cash equivalent is £20,000 x 29% = £5,800. Employers' NI on this will be £742.40 (£5,800 x 12.8%) payable by July 6, 2007. Of course if you only have the car for part of the tax year the cash equivalent value is scaled down accordingly.

NI on private fuel. The company will also have to pay employers' NI on the cash equivalent value of any fuel it provides for your private mileage - such as driving between home and work. Unless you are doing a high number of private miles in your company car, it's probably not worth letting the company pay for your fuel. So when you pick up your new company car from the dealer make sure that you personally pay for any fuel in the vehicle that's included in the delivery price. By the time you get home you will have used the fuel for a private journey, leaving yourself open to be taxed (and your company NI'd)!

Private fuel benefit. Since April 6, 2003 fuel provided for private use has been taxed using the CO_2 emissions figure of the vehicle. The same taxable percentage used to calculate the company car benefit is applied to a set figure of £14,400 to calculate the tax charge for fuel used for private mileage. The good news was that the existing (2002/03) all-or-nothing rule was also scrapped, so if you stop taking free fuel during the year, the tax charge is reduced in proportion to the period you do not receive it.

Example.

> Your company car has a CO_2 emissions figure of 210gr/km so you are taxed on 29% of its list price in 2005/06. If the company pays for fuel on your private journeys for the entire tax year you will also be taxed on £4,176 (29% x £14,400). The employers' NI bill would be £534.25 (£4,176 x 12.8%).

COMPANY CARS

© PROFIT EXTRACTION, Indicator

SHOULD THE COMPANY DEDUCT TAX?

Tax. The company is not required to deduct tax directly from the value of the car. The tax due is collected through your tax code and the Pay-As-You-Earn (PAYE) system, so you pay tax on the cash equivalent value of the car each week/month.

Telling the Taxman. The company must inform the Taxman that its' provided you with a company car by completing Form P46 (Car) when it's first made available. This form, completed for all cars provided by the company, should normally be sent to the Taxman once per quarter, but in order to speed up the system send them in as soon they're ready.

WHAT ABOUT RUNNING COSTS?

The company can claim a tax deduction for all running costs, including insurance, car tax, repair and servicing costs.

To work out the non-tax cost to your company of running a car have a look at the free service provided on the AA website. The AA take their information from a variety of sources to arrive at the standing and running costs of a car (see http://www.theaa.com/allaboutcars/advice/advice_rcosts_home.html).

DOES IT MATTER HOW MUCH THE COMPANY PAYS FOR THE CAR?

Supercar. If the car cost more than £12,000, the amount the company can deduct for tax purposes will be restricted, as discussed above. If the company buys a really expensive car that costs over £80,000 the list price is taken as £80,000 rather than the higher actual list price. The maximum cash equivalent for a company car is thus £28,000 (35% x 80,000).

Example.

> *If your company provides you with an Aston Martin DB7 that costs £109,000 you would pay income tax of £11,200 (£28,000 x 40%) per year as a 40% taxpayer. The employers' NI cost on this would be £3,584 (£28,000 x 12.8%). If it weren't for the cap on the list price your income tax bill would be £15,260 (£109,000 x 35% = £38,150 x 40%) per year.*

Classic car. If the car is over 15 years old at the end of the tax year it is officially classified as a classic car for tax purposes. If the current market value of the classic car is also more than £15,000 this must be used to calculate the taxable benefit-in-kind figure, rather than the original list price. However, if the car is worth less than £15,000 the original list price is used, which can produce a significant tax saving.

ENGINE SIZE	REGISTERED PRE-1998 (ALL FUEL TYPES)
1,400cc OR LESS	15%
1,401cc TO 2,000cc	22%
OVER 2,000cc OR NO CYLINDER CAPACITY	32%

COMPANY CARS

Example.

A 1963 MGB Roadster that originally cost £500, is now worth £8,000. It has no CO_2 emissions figure, so the cash equivalent value is based on its engine size and the original list price i.e. benefit-in-kind £110 (22% x £500). At the top tax rate of 40% you would pay tax of just £44 per year for using the MGB Roadster as a company car. Employers' NI would only be £14.08 (£110 x 12.8%).

© PROFIT EXTRACTION, Indicator

SECTION 3: YOU

SHOULD A COMPANY CAR BE SHOWN ON YOUR TAX RETURN?

The company car is a benefit from your employment with the company so you should complete the "Employment" pages of your tax return. The cash equivalent value of the company car must be included in the section headed "Benefits and Expenses". The figure to use will be shown on the annual Return of Expenses and Benefits (Form P11D) completed by the company for you each tax year. The company has to give you a copy of Form P11D or a list of the entries included on it by July 6 each year.

Tax codes. You should, however, check your PAYE notice of coding to ensure that the cash equivalent value of your company car has been included. You should also check that the amount shown is correct. It is not unknown for the Taxman to make an error.

CAN YOU DEDUCT ANY EXPENSES?

You cannot deduct expenses from the cash equivalent value of the company car, which is the amount you are taxed on.

WHAT IS THE NI COST?

Employees' NI. You do not pay NI on the cash equivalent value of the company car. Only the company has to pay NI on this benefit-in-kind.

AT WHAT RATE WILL YOU BE TAXED?

Marginal rate. The rate of tax that applies to the cash equivalent value of your company car depends on your total income during the tax year.

IS ANY TAX PAYABLE IN ADVANCE?

PAYE. You do not pay tax on the company car before it is made available to you. The tax due on the cash equivalent value of it should be deducted from your salary gradually through the PAYE system while you are using the car.

However, if you were provided with a company car late during the tax year, or the amount of cash equivalent value for the car included in your tax code was incorrect, there may be more tax to pay. If the additional tax due is more than £2,000 it must be paid by January 31. If it is less than £2,000 and you submitted your tax return in good time, the extra tax will be collected through the PAYE system in the following tax year.

COMPANY CARS

SECTION 4: VAT

ARE THERE ANY CONSEQUENCES FOR VAT?

You. There are no VAT consequences for you.

Your company. The general rule is that you are blocked from recovering the input VAT on the purchase of a car. However, you can claim the VAT element of a regular lease payment. Although if the leased car has any private use (and most do) you are only allowed to claim 50% of the input VAT.

With contract hire you can opt for other services such as a maintenance contract, roadside assistance etc. Ask the hire company to split these out on the invoice so that you can claim back the input VAT on these.

If the company arranges for maintenance of the leased car it can claim 100% of the VAT on the running costs such as servicing, tyres, repairs etc. There is no 50% input VAT restriction on these costs.

© PROFIT EXTRACTION, Indicator

SECTION 5: EXAMPLE

This is an example of the tax-related consequences of having a car provided by your company.

We first look at what the company must pay in Corporation Tax (CT) to have net profits available to provide the car. We will then calculate the net amount that you will be left with as an individual after deduction of income tax.

We have used the following assumptions:

List price of company car	£21,500
CO_2 emissions rating of company car	235 gr/km
Percentage of the car's list price which is taxable	34%
CT rate paid by company	19%
Employers' NI rate	12.8%
Your highest income tax rate	40%
Annual leasing costs of the car	£4,200
Car tax	£160
Insurance	£600
Servicing, tyres and repairs	£640
Total cost of providing a company car	£5,600

Disallowed leasing cost. First step, excess over £12,000 = £21,500 - £12,000 = £9,500. Second step, proportion of list price £9,500/21,500 = 44%. Third step, take half of this as the percentage. Finally, disallowed leasing cost is 22% x £4,200 leasing cost = £924.

COMPANY'S TAX POSITION			
	£	£	CT PAYABLE
PROFITS MADE BY THE COMPANY		70,000.00	13,300.00
COST OF PROVIDING THE COMPANY CAR *(SEE ABOVE)*	5,600.00	-5,600.00	
DISALLOWED LEASING COST *(SEE ABOVE)*		924.00	
EMPLOYERS' NI ON TAXABLE BENEFIT *(12.8% x £7,310 - SEE BELOW)*	935.68	-935.68	
TAXABLE PROFITS		64,388.32	12,233.78
CT SAVED BY PAYING FOR A CAR	-1,066.22		-1,066.22
NET COST FOR THE COMPANY *(COSTS LESS CT SAVED)*	5,469.46		

NET COST AS A PERCENTAGE OF THE COST OF PROVIDING THE CAR	97.66%

COMPANY CARS

© PROFIT EXTRACTION, Indicator

YOUR TAX POSITION			
TAX YEAR ENDED APRIL 5, 2006	**£**	**£**	**%**
VALUE OF THE CAR TO YOU*		5,600.00	100%
BUT THE TAXABLE BENEFIT OF HAVING THE COMPANY CAR IS (TAXABLE PERCENTAGE OF 34% MULTIPLIED BY THE LIST PRICE OF £21,500)	7,310.00		
INCOME TAX DUE AT 40% (ON £7,310)		-2,924.00	52%
NET VALUE OF CAR PROVIDED		2,676.00	48%

*To work out the net value to you of having the car provided we have assumed that it would cost you the same amount to lease, service, tax and insure as it would the company.

COMPANY CARS

© PROFIT EXTRACTION, indicator

SECTION 6: PROS & CONS

ADVANTAGES OF A COMPANY CAR

1. No hassle. When the company provides you with a car all the hassle of car ownership is removed. You don't have to worry about servicing, the cost of repairs or insurance. The company also takes on the burden of a loan or lease to acquire the car, and will supply a replacement when you need one.

2. No employees' NI. You do not have to pay NI on the cash equivalent value of the company car, although you do pay income tax on that amount.

3. Share the benefit. The company can provide members of your family or household with company cars to use as they wish. You will be taxed on the cash equivalent value of those cars, but it can be more tax-efficient for the company to provide small, fuel-efficient cars, rather than pay you extra salary to buy those cars personally.

4. Reduce Corporation Tax. When the company incurs the expense of a company car it reduces the profits subject to Corporation Tax. This is particularly the case when the car has an official CO_2 emissions figure of 120 gr/km or less and was purchased on or after April 16, 2002.

5. Fuel-only mileage. The company can pay you a tax-free mileage rate for using the company car for business-related journeys, if it does not also provide you with free fuel for those journeys (see Part 8).

DISADVANTAGES OF A COMPANY CAR

1. Employers' NI. The company must pay employers' NI at 12.8% on the cash equivalent value of the company car.

2. Cash equivalent. The value of the cash equivalent, which is the amount you pay tax on, may be greater than the cost of providing the car.

3. Fuel. The cash equivalent value of free fuel provided for private use in a company car is very high. It will not be tax-efficient to have free fuel provided by the company unless you drive a higher than average number of non-business related miles during the year.

4. Capital cost restricted. The company cannot deduct the full cost of the car in the year of purchase, unless the vehicle is a new low-emissions car purchased on or after April 16, 2002 and before April 1, 2008. The full cost is tax-deductible but it must be spread over the period the car is owned.

5. Leasing deduction restricted. If the retail price of the car is more than £12,000 the full cost of the lease is not tax-deductible for the company. The leasing costs must also be spread evenly over the period of the lease although the company may pay much of the cost up-front.

6. VAT. The company cannot reclaim VAT on the cost of buying a company car. If the company leases the car it can reclaim only 50% of the VAT charged as part of the leasing fee.

COMPANY CARS

Profit Extraction

Mileage claims

SECTION 1: METHOD

WHAT IS A MILEAGE ALLOWANCE?

A mileage allowance is the amount paid by the company to an employer or a director who uses their own or a company vehicle for journeys connected with business. The allowance may be a flat rate per mile driven, or a sum paid to cover all the business journeys to be made in a set period.

HOW DO YOU WITHDRAW A MILEAGE ALLOWANCE?

Expense claims. The mileage allowance can be paid by cash, cheque or by transfer to your private bank account. A flat rate per mile should only be paid after you have submitted expense claims to the company that show the number of miles driven on business journeys.

Lump sum. Something that might be more administratively convenient is paying a lump sum. This can be paid annually or in monthly or weekly instalments. However, it must be paid before the end of the tax year.

HOW MUCH MILEAGE ALLOWANCE CAN YOU WITHDRAW?

Tax-free limit only. There is no legal limit on the amount of mileage allowance you can withdraw from the company. You can take as little or as much as you like. However, the allowance will only be tax and NI-free if it is: (1) paid for business journeys; and (2) paid at or below the statutory rate. If the company pays you a mileage allowance at a higher rate, the excess will be taxed as if it were a bonus payment (see Part 2).

Lump sum. If the company pays you a lump sum as a mileage allowance it will be tax-free if the total value of such allowances paid during the tax year is less than or equal to the amount you would have received at statutory mileage rates. Any amounts paid in excess of the statutory rate will be taxable.

Example.

> The company pays you a lump sum of £1,000 per year for using your own car for business journeys plus 25p per mile. You drive 8,000 miles on business in the tax year, meaning a payment of 8,000 miles x 25p = £2,000. Total mileage allowance paid: £3,000. The statutory rate is 40p per mile, so the total tax-free amount for the year is 8,000 x 40p = £3,200. The total actually paid of £3,000 is less than the amount that could be paid at the statutory rate, so the full mileage allowance, including the lump sum is tax-free.

© PROFIT EXTRACTION, Indicator

SECTION 2: YOUR COMPANY

IS A MILEAGE ALLOWANCE TAX-DEDUCTIBLE?

A mileage allowance paid to a director or employee will always be tax-deductible for the company if it is paid in respect of business journeys. Even if the amount paid exceeds the statutory rates, the company will still be able to set the full allowance paid against its profits.

Business journeys. Travel to and from your home and your permanent office at the company site will not be a business journey, but travelling to see customers or to a temporary workplace can be business-related. A workplace will be temporary if you plan to, and actually do work there for less than 24 months. If the company has various sites, travelling between them will always be business-related.

Associated companies. If you are a director of several companies you may be required to travel between them during the working day. That travel is regarded as a business journey if the companies are all in the same group. However, if they are unrelated, your travel between them is classed as a private journey and so not tax-deductible.

WHICH MILEAGE RATES SHOULD BE USED?

A mileage allowance is generally paid tax-free. But any allowance paid in excess of the statutory rate is taxable and attracts employees' and employers' NI. This increases the cost of the allowance paid by the company and reduces the net amount payable to the individual.

Authorised rates. The statutory tax-free rates for using your own car, van, motorbike or bicycle for the business journey are:

STATUTORY TAX-FREE RATES		
	FIRST 10,000 BUSINESS MILES	BUSINESS MILES IN EXCESS OF 10,000
CAR OR VAN	40P PER MILE	25P PER MILE
MOTORBIKE	24P PER MILE	24P PER MILE
BICYCLE	20P PER MILE	20P PER MILE

Fuel-only. If the company provides you with a car but no fuel, it can pay you a fuel-only tax-free mileage rate according to the car engine size and fuel type:

FUEL-ONLY RATES			
ENGINE SIZE	PETROL	DIESEL	LPG
1,400CC OR LESS	10P PER MILE	9P PER MILE	7P PER MILE
1,401 TO 2000CC	12P PER MILE	9P PER MILE	8P PER MILE
OVER 2000CC	14P PER MILE	12P PER MILE	10P PER MILE

These fuel-only rates are not statutory and can be negotiated upwards if your company car has a large engine or achieves fewer than 17 miles to the gallon. If this is the case get the Taxman to agree in writing to a special rate applicable to your car.

MILEAGE CLAIMS

Passengers. If another employee or director needs to undertake the same business journey, it makes sense to take only one car. The company can pay you an extra tax-free mileage allowance of 5p per mile per additional passenger carried. This passenger mileage allowance can be paid if you are driving your own or a company car.

WHAT IF THE COMPANY PAYS TOO MUCH?

NI. If part of the mileage allowance is taxable (i.e. in excess of the tax-free rates) the company will have to pay over employees' and employers' NI on that part. So that the correct amount of NI can be calculated on this excess, the company must add the taxable element to your earnings in the month the allowance was paid.

Income tax. If part of the mileage allowance is taxable, the company must include that amount on your Form P11D for the tax year and give you details of the amounts reported by July 6. Apart from this situation, any statutory mileage rate payments are excluded from P11D reporting.

© PROFIT EXTRACTION, Indicator

SECTION 3: YOU

SHOULD THIS BE SHOWN ON YOUR TAX RETURN?

If the whole of the mileage allowance paid is tax-free it does not have to be reported on your tax return. Copy any taxable mileage allowance payments from your Form P11D, the company gives you, on to the "Employment" pages of your tax return in the section titled "Benefits and Expenses".

CAN YOU DEDUCT ANY EXPENSES FOR UNPAID MILEAGE?

Own car. If the company has paid you a mileage allowance that is less than the statutory rate, you can claim the difference as a deduction from your other income on your tax return. This only applies to mileage rates paid for business journeys in your own vehicle. It does not apply to the passenger mileage rate or the fuel-only mileage rates.

Example.

> You travel 7,000 business miles in the tax year in your own car and the company pays you a mileage allowance of 35p per mile.

MILEAGE ALLOWANCE PAID	*7,000 MILES X 35P*	*£2,450*
STATUTORY MILEAGE RATE	*7,000 MILES X 40P*	*£2,800*
CLAIM ON YOUR TAX RETURN	*7,000 X (40 - 35)P*	*£350*

AT WHAT RATE IS EXCESS MILEAGE TAXED?

Highest rate. If the mileage allowance is paid in excess of the statutory rates so part of it is taxable, that part will be reported on Form P11D and on your tax return. The additional tax due will be paid as part of your self-assessment tax calculation prepared either by the Taxman or you when your tax return is completed. The tax paid will be at your highest rate.

MILEAGE CLAIMS

SECTION 4: VAT

ARE THERE ANY CONSEQUENCES FOR VAT?

You. None.

Your company. The payment of the mileage allowance does not attract output VAT. The good news is that your company can claim back the VAT on the fuel element of the business mileage. It can do this either by working out the fuel efficiency of your individual car or using the fuel-only rates.

Example.

> You put in expense claims to your company for 8,000 business miles in the tax year, which the company duly pays at the rate of 40p per mile. VAT is also recoverable by your company on this transaction. However, only on fuel paid for, not on the full 40p per mile. Using a fuel-only rate of say 12p per mile this gives the company a fuel cost of £960 (8,000 x 12p). The recoverable VAT on this is £960 x (17.5 /117.5) = £142.98. The company can claim this input VAT via its VAT return.

> The VATman has approved the use of the fuel-only rate to reclaim VAT on fuel forming part of business mileage expense claims.

© PROFIT EXTRACTION, Indicator

MILEAGE CLAIMS

SECTION 5: EXAMPLE

This is an example of the tax-related consequences of withdrawing a mileage allowance from your company.

We first look at what the payment of the mileage claim costs your company in net terms. We are taking into account the fact that the payment is tax-deductible for the company. We will then calculate the net amount that you will be left with as an individual after deduction of income tax.

We have used the following assumptions:

Business miles driven	20,000
Mileage rates paid for business miles	40p or 25p per mile
Corporation Tax (CT) rate paid by company	19%

COMPANY'S TAX POSITION			
	£	£	CT PAYABLE
PROFITS MADE BY THE COMPANY		70,000.00	13,300.00
MILEAGE PAID (10,000 MILES X 40P AND 10,000 MILES X 25P)	6,500.00	-6,500.00	
TAXABLE PROFITS		63,500.00	12,065.00
CT SAVED (£6,500 x 19%)	-1,235.00		-1,235.00
NET COST TO THE COMPANY (COST LESS CT SAVED)	5,265.00		

NET COST AS A PERCENTAGE OF MILEAGE CLAIM PAID	81%

YOUR TAX POSITION			
TAX YEAR ENDED APRIL 5, 2006	£	£	
MILEAGE ALLOWANCE	6,500.00	6,500.00	100%
TAX-FREE FOR FIRST 10,000 MILES (AT 40P)	-4,000.00		
TAX-FREE AMOUNT ON NEXT 10,000 MILES (AT 25P)	-2,500.00		
INCOME TAX ON MILEAGE ALLOWANCE		-	0%
NET ALLOWANCE		6,500.00	100%

SECTION 6: PROS & CONS

ADVANTAGES OF A MILEAGE ALLOWANCE

1. Tax and NI-free. Mileage allowances paid within the statutory rates are free of tax and NI.

2. Simple. The calculation of a mileage allowance is very simple for your own car. It is paid at the same rate for every size of engine and irrespective of the type of fuel it runs on.

3. Passengers. You can receive up to 5p per mile tax-free for each employee you carry as a passenger on a business journey, whether in your own or a company car.

4. Company car. The company can pay you a tax-free fuel-only mileage allowance for business journeys made in the company car.

5. No reporting. You do not have to keep receipts for fuel or repairs and you do not have to report a tax-free mileage allowance on your tax return.

DISADVANTAGES OF A MILEAGE ALLOWANCE

1. Accurate records. You must keep accurate records of the business journeys undertaken which the mileage allowance is paid for. You must also record when and how many passengers you carried.

2. Not for travelling to work. A mileage allowance will only be tax-free if it's paid for business journeys. Travelling between your home and the office is not generally a business journey.

3. Penalises high business mileage. If you drive a large number of business miles in your own car the tax-free mileage allowance will not fully reimburse you for the running costs of the car on those journeys over the 10,000 mile threshold.

4. Non-business journeys? It can be difficult to work out whether a journey is a business journey if you are travelling to a temporary workplace.

5. NI administration. The company must keep track of the mileage allowance paid each month and add the taxable amount to earnings to work out the employees' and employers' NI due (if any).

© PROFIT EXTRACTION, Indicator

Profit Extraction

Personal pensions

SECTION 1: METHOD

WHAT IS A PERSONAL PENSION CONTRIBUTION?

You may normally pay a regular portion of your salary, or a lump sum into a pension scheme. This is known as a pension contribution. Your company can pay this pension contribution on your behalf although the amount will be limited by a number of factors such as the type of pension scheme and your age. In this part of the book we assume that it's a personal pension scheme or a stakeholder pension scheme.

HOW SHOULD THE CONTRIBUTION BE PAID?

The company could pay the pension contribution directly to the pension company giving the reference number of your scheme. A pension contribution paid this way is treated as a gross contribution, meaning there's no additional tax rebate if you're a 40% taxpayer.

WHAT IS THE MAXIMUM THAT CAN BE PAID THIS WAY?

There is a limit on how much can be paid into your pension scheme each year. This limit is a percentage of your earnings. Some types of income such as dividends or interest, do not count as earnings. The salary you receive from your company will be earnings as will the value of any benefits-in-kind. Your relevant earnings are those for the tax year less allowable expenses such as a claim for an approved mileage allowance.

The maximum pension contribution that can be made varies according to how old you were at the beginning of the tax year, as follows:

AGE (AT 5/4/05)	35 OR UNDER	36 TO 45	46 TO 50	51 TO 55	56 TO 60	61 OR MORE
PERCENTAGE*	17.5%	20%	25%	30%	35%	40%

*Percentage is of net relevant earnings for the tax year.

Example.

> *You were aged 40 on April 5, 2005 and earn £50,000 p.a. Using the table there is a maximum of £10,000 (20% x £50,000) that can be paid into pension schemes for 2005/06.*

Capped. Your earnings for pension puposes are also capped at a maximum amount (£105,600 for 2005/06) with any excess being ignored.

No earnings. The above limits are ignored for the first £3,600 (gross) of pension contributions you pay in each tax year. This means pension contributions of up to this amount can be paid irrespective of the level of your income.

Any contribution paid by your company into your pension scheme must be deducted from the maximum contributions you are permitted to pay for that tax year.

PERSONAL PENSIONS

© PROFIT EXTRACTION, Indicator

SECTION 2: YOUR COMPANY

TAX-DEDUCTIBLE FOR THE COMPANY?

Yes. Pension contributions paid on behalf of employees and directors into an approved pension scheme are tax-deductible. An approved pension scheme is one that has been authorised by the Taxman. All stakeholder pension schemes and personal pension schemes run by assurance companies should be approved.

Deductible in which financial year? A pension contribution is tax-deductible in the financial year it is paid and not the tax year it gets added to your pension scheme.

Example.

In 2005 your company makes a £55,000 profit so you decide that it should pay a £5,000 contribution into your pension scheme. This means that your company will be taxed on only £50,000.

Condition. For the pension contribution to be tax-deductible it must be paid before the company's year-end.

If the company draws up its accounts to December 31, 2005, any pension contribution for 2005 must be paid by December 31 to be set against the profits made in the 2005 set of accounts. A contribution is therefore an ideal way to reduce the taxable profit of the company before the financial year-end has passed.

WHAT IS THE NI COST?

None. The pension contributions paid by the company are not subject to employers' NI.

HOW MUCH CAN BE PAID?

There is a limit on how much can be paid into a pension scheme each year. This limit is a percentage of the scheme member's earnings.

The limits on how much pension contribution paid in a tax year are important. If the contribution exceeds the maximum permitted, the excess must be returned to the payer.

PERSONAL PENSIONS

SECTION 3: YOU

SHOULD THE PENSION CONTRIBUTION BE SHOWN ON YOUR TAX RETURN?

The pension contribution paid by your company should not be shown on your tax return.

CAN YOU DEDUCT ANY EXPENSES FROM A PENSION CONTRIBUTION?

As the pension contribution paid by your company is not treated as your income, expenses paid by you cannot be deducted from it.

WHAT IS THE NI COST?

None. The contribution paid into an approved pension scheme by your company is not treated as your income, so no income tax or employees' NI is due.

AT WHAT RATE WILL A PENSION CONTRIBUTION FINALLY BE TAXED?

A pension contribution made by your company is not taxable on you. When you eventually receive a pension from the pension scheme, that will be taxed. However, this may well be a time when you are only a 22% taxpayer rather than taxed at higher rates, so you'd gain that way.

SECTION 4: VAT

ARE THERE ANY CONSEQUENCES FOR VAT?

None. There are no VAT consequences.

SECTION 5: EXAMPLE

This is an example of the tax-related consequences of having the company make a pension contribution on your behalf.

We first look at what the payment of the pension contribution costs your company in net terms. We are taking into account the fact that the pension contribution is tax-deductible for the company.

As the pension contribution is not paid directly to you, there is no effect on your personal tax position. However, if the pension contribution paid by the company replaces a contribution you would normally pay out of your net salary, you will be left with more money to spend.

We have used the following assumptions:

Pension contribution paid by the company	£5,000
Corporation Tax (CT) rate paid by the company	19%
Your highest personal tax rate	40%

COMPANY'S TAX POSITION			
	£	**£**	**CT PAYABLE**
TAXABLE PROFIT IN THE COMPANY BEFORE DEDUCTION OF THE GROSS PENSION CONTRIBUTION		70,000.00	13,300.00
GROSS PENSION CONTRIBUTION	5,000.00	-5,000.00	
NET PROFIT AFTER CONTRIBUTION		65,000.00	12,350.00
CT SAVED BY PAYING THE PENSION CONTRIBUTION	-950.00		-950.00
NET COST TO THE COMPANY *(COST LESS CT SAVED)*	4,050.00		

NET COST AS A PERCENTAGE OF THE PENSION CONTRIBUTION	81%

© PROFIT EXTRACTION, indicator

SECTION 6: PROS & CONS

ADVANTAGES OF A PERSONAL PENSION CONTRIBUTION

1. NI saved. When the company pays a contribution into your pension scheme it is free of NI. If you pay the same contribution yourself the amount paid must be deducted from your earnings after NI has been charged. So a pension contribution paid by the company saves employees' as well as employers' NI.

2. No tax. You are not taxed on the pension contribution the company pays on your behalf into your pension scheme.

3. Reduces Corporation Tax. The pension contribution is tax-deductible for the company.

4. Diversion. The company can pay a pension contribution on behalf of your spouse or other relatives into a stakeholder pension scheme set up in their name, as long as the maximum contribution limit is not exceeded for each individual. The contributions paid for individuals who are not employees of the company will not be tax-deductible, but the individuals for whom the contributions are paid will not be taxed on them.

DISADVANTAGES OF A PERSONAL PENSION CONTRIBUTION

1. Limited amount. The amount of pension contribution that may be paid by the company is limited by the maximum permitted contribution for the tax year. This maximum figure is calculated as a percentage (depending on your age at the beginning of the tax year) of your net relevant earnings for the entire tax year.

2. Affects personal contributions. Any pension contribution paid by the company on your behalf must be deducted from the maximum pension contribution payable for that tax year. This leaves you less scope to make a pension contribution yourself in the same tax year.

3. No additional income. A pension contribution does not increase your income in the year it is paid.

4. Locked-in funds. The amount paid as a pension contribution is locked into your pension scheme until you reach the permitted retirement age for that scheme. You have no control over those funds in the meantime.

5. Charges. The amount paid as a pension contribution may be eroded by annual charges imposed by the company which runs the scheme.

PERSONAL PENSIONS

Profit Extraction

Using company assets

SECTION 1: METHOD

WHAT IS MEANT BY USING COMPANY ASSETS?

The company can buy an asset, say a computer or a hi-fi, and let you use it in your own home with no restriction. Generally you will be taxed on 20% of its value but there are special rules for certain assets. If your family also uses the asset there is no additional tax charge.

Special rules. We have already looked at the tax rules surrounding company cars (see Part 7). Other special rules can be found in the Inland Revenue Booklet "Employees Expenses and Benefits", which is available from the Employers' Orderline on 08457 646646; or from the Taxman's website http://www.hmrc.gov.uk/employers.

Additional services. If the company pays for additional services which allow you to use the asset, such as an Internet connection or mooring fees for a boat, you will also be taxed on the cost of such services. So keep an eye on these too.

WHAT NEEDS TO HAPPEN?

The company should purchase the asset in its own name, retain ownership, insure and maintain it.

Not a gift. If the company gives you the asset you will be taxed as if you had received a bonus equal to its market value on the date it was transferred.

DOES IT MATTER HOW MUCH THE ASSET IS WORTH?

Yes. The tax you pay is based on the value of the asset. The higher the value the more tax there is to pay.

USING COMPANY ASSETS

© PROFIT EXTRACTION, Indicator

SECTION 2: YOUR COMPANY

IS THE PROVISION OF ASSETS TAX-DEDUCTIBLE FOR THE COMPANY?

The cost of providing the asset is tax deductible for the company. There are no special rules just because you use the asset. The general rule that the full purchase price of the asset cannot be deducted from the company's profits in one year still applies.

40% in the first year. Companies which are medium-sized or smaller can claim a 40% tax deduction for the cost of assets in the year of purchase and may deduct 25% of the remaining cost in subsequent years.

A medium-sized company is one that meets two of the following criteria: (1) turnover of no more than £22.8 million; (2) total asset value of no more than £11.4 million; (3) no more than 250 employees; or (4) it met these conditions in the previous accounting period.

A small company is one that meets at least two of the following criteria: (1) turnover of no more than £5.6 million; (2) total asset value of no more than £2.8 million; (3) less than 50 employees; or it met these conditions in the previous accounting period.

WHAT IS THE NI COST?

Employers' NI. When the company completes your annual Return of Expenses and Benefits (Form P11D) it must also complete a form P11D(b) and pay NI (by July 6) on the cash equivalent value of this benefit-in-kind at the rate of 12.8 %.

HOW DO YOU CALCULATE THE BENEFIT-IN-KIND?

When it's first provided. Your company has to calculate the cash equivalent value of you having use of the asset. The Taxman says this is equal to 20% of its value *"when first provided to you"*, plus any other costs the company incurs in providing the asset.

Example.

If the company purchases a new DVD player for £250 and immediately "lends" it to you to use at home, you are taxed on the cash equivalent value of £50 (£250 x 20%) for every year that you have use of the DVD player. If the company provides you with an old video player that cost £250 but is worth only £60 when you start to use it, you're taxed on the cash equivalent value of £12 per year (£60 x 20%).

So the annual cash equivalent value can be reduced if the company uses the asset for a little while before lending it to you, i.e. so that it depreciates in value.

USING COMPANY ASSETS

Made available. If the asset is only available for you to use for part of the year, the cash equivalent value can be reduced in proportion to the length of time during which you could use the asset. To get this reduction past the Taxman you will need documentation such as board minutes and a clause in your contract of employment that restricts the availability of the asset.

Business use. If the asset is used exclusively for your business at certain times, the cash equivalent value is reduced by the proportion that represents the business use.

Example.

> If the company provides you with a fax machine which cost £200, but 70% of your use of the machine is to relay instructions to staff at the company, the taxable cash equivalent value will be £12 per year; 30% private use x (£200 x 20%). If the business use of the asset is 90% or more any personal use is ignored, so you are not taxed on the provision of the asset.

Hired assets. If the company hires the asset rather than buys it outright, and the hire charge is at least 20% of the cost of the asset, the cash equivalent value that you are taxed on is the cost the company incurs and not the smaller sum of 20% of the value of the asset.

Example.

> The company hires a boat for £1,200 to be used by you and your family for a month. The boat is valued at £30,000 at the time. So 20% of the value is £6,000, which is reduced to £500 (6,000 x 1/12), as the boat is only available for one month. However, because the hire cost of £1,200 is greater you are taxed on that sum instead.

Tax-free computer. A home computer and the equipment attached to it, such as a printer, modem, or scanner, can be provided tax and NI-free to you as long as the total cost of the equipment is not more than £2,500.

However, this perk will not be tax-free if it's restricted to just you and your family - other employees must be able to ask the company to provide them with home computers too. Whilst the company does not have to provide every employee with a home computer, the Taxman must see that they are at least available to all staff.

© PROFIT EXTRACTION, indicator

SECTION 3: YOU

SHOULD THIS BE SHOWN ON YOUR TAX RETURN?

The cash equivalent value as shown on your Form P11D must be reported on your tax return on the "Employment" pages under the heading "Benefits and Expenses". If the provision of the asset is not taxable, such as a computer, you do not have to enter anything on your tax return.

CAN YOU DEDUCT ANY EXPENSES?

You can, if those expenses would normally be deductible from your salary, and they have not already been deducted from it (see Part 1).

Made good. Any money you pay to the company in return for using the asset can reduce the amount you are taxed on. This is known as making good.

WHAT IS THE NI COST TO YOU?

Employees' NI. You do not have to pay employees' NI on the cash equivalent of the asset provided.

AT WHAT RATE WILL YOU FINALLY BE TAXED?

Marginal rate. The top rate of tax that applies to your total income for the tax year.

SHOULD ANY TAX BE PAID IN ADVANCE?

You do not pay tax on the provision of the assets before it is made available to you. Any tax due on the cash equivalent value of the asset should be deducted from your salary every month under the PAYE system. This is after your tax code has been updated by the Taxman for this benefit-in-kind.

USING COMPANY ASSETS

SECTION 4: VAT

ARE THERE ANY CONSEQUENCES FOR VAT?

You. The 20% calculation is based on the VAT-inclusive value of the asset, even if the company has already successfully claimed back the input VAT on it. So your company needs to remember this when calculating the cash equivalent value.

Company. The input VAT suffered on any associated costs of, say, maintaining the assets would not be recoverable because of mixed (private and business) use. The general rule for VAT where there is mixed use is to claim just the business proportion of the input VAT through the company's VAT return.

© PROFIT EXTRACTION, Indicator

SECTION 5: EXAMPLE

Here is an example of the tax-related consequences of having an asset provided by your company. We look at what this costs your company, allowing for any tax deductions. We then calculate the amount of income tax you must pay for having the use of the asset.

We have used the following assumptions:

The company provides you with a furnished flat. The tax arising on the use of the flat is discussed in Part 11. However, the tax charge on the use of the furniture in the flat is shown below.

Market value of furniture when first provided to you	£2,500
Employers' NI rate	12.8%
Corporation Tax (CT) rate paid by company	19%
Your highest personal tax rate	40%

COMPANY'S TAX POSITION	£	£	CT PAYABLE
TAXABLE PROFIT IN COMPANY BEFORE PROVISION OF FURNITURE TO YOU		70,000.00	13,300.00
FURNITURE PROVIDED FOR THE FLAT	2,500.00		
TAX DEDUCTION FOR FURNITURE *(SPREAD OVER A NUMBER OF YEARS)*		-2,500.00	
EMPLOYERS' NI ON THE BENEFIT-IN-KIND *(20% OF £2,500 X 12.8%)*	64.00	-64.00	
NET PROFIT		67,436.00	12,812.84
CT SAVED *(OVER A NUMBER OF YEARS)* BY PROVIDING FURNITURE	-487.16		-487.16
NET COST TO THE COMPANY *(COSTS LESS CT SAVED)*	2,076.84		

NET COST AS A PERCENTAGE OF THE OUTLAY ON FURNITURE	83.07%

YOUR TAX POSITION	£	£	%
FURNITURE YOU DIDN'T HAVE TO BUY		2,500.00	100%
CASH EQUIVALENT OF THE FURNITURE *(20% X £2,500 EACH YEAR)*	500.00		
INCOME TAX AT 40% *(ON £500)*		-200.00	8%
NET INCREASE IN YOUR POSITION		2,300.00	92%

SECTION 6: PROS & CONS

ADVANTAGES OF USING COMPANY ASSETS

1. Saving employees' NI. There is no employees' NI for you to pay on this benefit-in-kind.

2. Computer. Computer equipment worth up to £2,500 can be provided with no tax or NI charges arising. If the cost of the equipment exceeds £2,500 only the excess is taxed.

3. Tax deductible. The company can deduct the cost of providing an asset to an employee from its profits, even if it's not used in the business.

4. Taxed on only 20% of the value. Instead of being taxed and NI'd on the full value of an asset if the company gave it to you, you only pay tax on 20% of the value each tax year.

DISADVANTAGES OF USING COMPANY ASSETS

1. Five-year limit. If you keep the asset for more than five years you will be taxed on more than it originally cost.

2. Made available. You are taxed on the cash equivalent value of the asset whether or not you actually use it during the year. If the asset is available for you to use, you're taxed on it.

3. Employers' NI. If you are taxed on the provision of the asset the company will pay employers' NI on the cash equivalent value that appears on your P11D.

4. Sale restrictions. You will not own the asset the company provides, so you will not have the freedom to sell or change it if it is unsuitable.

© PROFIT EXTRACTION, Indicator

Profit Extraction

Free accommodation

SECTION 1: METHOD

WHAT IS MEANT BY FREE ACCOMMODATION?

The company can provide you with living accommodation either through a property for your use which it owns, or by leasing a property and allowing you to use it. The accommodation described in this part of the book is long-term, rather than board and lodging (which would be provided in a hotel or guest house while you are staying away from home on a temporary basis).

HOW SHOULD THE ACCOMMODATION BE PROVIDED?

Not a gift. The company should retain ownership of the property. If the company gives you the property and puts your name on the deeds, you will be taxed as if you'd received a bonus equal to the market value of the property on the date it was transferred.

Lease. If the property is owned by a third party, the company should take out the lease in its own name, and arrange a sub-lease to allow you to use it. If you sign the lease in your own name and the company reimburses you for the rent and associated costs an additional NI charge will arise.

Free of charge. The company can provide the accommodation absolutely free with no strings attached, or it could ask you to pay some rent. Any rent you pay will reduce the amount you are taxed on (the cash equivalent value), for using the property. In either case it's prudent to have a lease agreement drawn up between you and the company which sets out who is responsible for meeting the expenses connected with the property, such as the Council Tax, repairs and mains services.

Shared. If your family also uses the property there is no additional tax charge. If other employees of the company use the same property in the same tax year the annual cash equivalent value for the use of the accommodation is split between all those who use it.

Documentation. It's best to get this sharing arrangement recorded in the company minutes and included in the relevant employee's contract of employment. This is particularly so if the accommodation is only available for use for part of the year, as the cash equivalent value can be reduced in proportion to the length of time during which it's not available. For example, if the company says you can only use the property for 20 days a year, then that's all you will be taxed on.

Furnished. The property may be provided furnished or unfurnished, but who owns the furniture will make a difference to the tax you pay. If the company owns it you will be taxed on its use in addition to the annual cash equivalent value assigned for using the property itself. The tax charge that applies for the use of furniture is described in Part 10.

DOES IT MATTER HOW MUCH THE PROPERTY IS WORTH?

How much the property is worth while you are living there is not necessarily important. You are taxed on an annual amount known as the cash equivalent value.

© PROFIT EXTRACTION, Indicator

SECTION 2: YOUR COMPANY

IS PROVIDING ACCOMMODATION TAX-DEDUCTIBLE FOR THE COMPANY?

Where the company pays rent for accommodation provided for your use as a director, it and any associated services are tax-deductible.

If the company owns the accommodation any running costs it pays in connection with the property such as repairs and water rates, are also tax-deductible. However, a tax deduction for the cost of any improvements to the property is only available when the property is disposed of.

HOW DO YOU CALCULATE THE VALUE OF FREE ACCOMMODATION?

Your company has to calculate the annual value of the free accommodation, known as the cash equivalent value. The calculation of this depends on the type of property as follows:

PROPERTY	CASH EQUIVALENT VALUE
COST LESS THAN £75,000	GROSS RATEABLE VALUE
COST MORE THAN £75,000	GROSS RATEABLE VALUE PLUS A NOMINAL RENT
SITUATED OVERSEAS IRRESPECTIVE OF COST	LOCAL MARKET RENT IF LET UNFURNISHED
IS RENTED BY THE COMPANY	RENT PAID BY THE COMPANY
IS OWNED BY A PERSON CONNECTED WITH YOU AND	MARKET RENT IRRESPECTIVE OF THE
RENTED BY THE COMPANY	ACTUAL RENT PAID

The terms used in the table above are explained as follows:

Cost. The cost of the property is normally what the company originally paid for it plus the cost of any improvements made before you start living there. However, if the cost including improvements was more than £75,000, and the company owned the property for more than six years before you started living there, the cost is replaced with the property's market value at the date you first occupied it, in the calculation of the cash equivalent value.

Gross rateable value. The local authority may not keep a list of the old rateable values of domestic properties in the area, as the Council Tax band is now the only figure relevant. So ask the District Valuers' office to supply the figure of gross rateable value. If the property has no rateable value you can use a reasonable estimate.

Nominal rent. The nominal rent is calculated as the excess of the property cost (or market value where substituted) over £75,000 multiplied by the official interest rate, which is currently set at 5%.

Example.

> The property cost the company £100,000, so the nominal rent is calculated as:
> (£100,000 - £75,000) x 5% = £1,250.

Market rent. This is the rent that would be obtained by a third party if the property were let on the open market.

FREE ACCOMMODATION

Business use. If part of the property is used exclusively for the company's business, for example as a storeroom, the cash equivalent value can be reduced by the proportion not used for business.

Example.

> *If the property provided has ten rooms and one room is used exclusively for business, an amount equal to one tenth of the cash equivalent value can be deducted as an expense on your tax return.*

WHAT IS THE NI COST?

Employers' NI. The company must pay NI at 12.8% on the cash equivalent value of the accommodation. This NI charge is paid annually by July 6 following the end of the tax year during which the accommodation was provided.

© PROFIT EXTRACTION, Indicator

SECTION 3: YOU

SHOULD THIS BE SHOWN ON YOUR TAX RETURN?

There are very few circumstances in which accommodation provided by your company is tax-free, and so it should normally be shown on your tax return.

Where the annual cash equivalent value of the accommodation is taxable, it should be shown on the "Employment" pages of your tax return in the section titled "Benefits and expenses".

P11D info. The cash equivalent value of the free accommodation should be calculated by your company and shown on your P11D which it has to prepare for each tax year. The company must provide you with a copy of the information on the P11D by July 6.

CAN YOU DEDUCT ANY EXPENSES?

Contribution. Any contribution you make towards the cost of the accommodation is deductible from the cash equivalent figure.

Use of home as office. The Taxman will only agree that the expenses for a home office are deductible if you have no other space available on the company's premises from which to conduct your business.

WHAT IS THE NI COST?

None. You do not have to pay employees' NI on the annual cash equivalent value of the accommodation provided by the company.

AT WHAT RATE WILL THIS FINALLY BE TAXED?

The cash equivalent value of the accommodation provided by the company will be taxed as if it were part of your total taxable income, meaning your top rate of tax applies.

IS ANY TAX PAYABLE IMMEDIATELY?

No. You do not pay tax on the accommodation before it is made available to you. The tax due on the cash equivalent value of the accommodation provided should be deducted from your salary every month through the Pay-As-You-Earn system. This is once the Taxman has updated your tax code for this benefit-in-kind.

FREE ACCOMMODATION

SECTION 4: VAT

ARE THERE ANY CONSEQUENCES FOR VAT?

Furnishings. The recovery of input VAT on accommodation is blocked if it's for a director. For other employees, claim for the proportion that's for business use.

© PROFIT EXTRACTION, Indicator

SECTION 5: EXAMPLE

Here is an example of the tax related consequences of having free living accommodation provided by your company.

We look at what the accommodation costs your company in net terms, assuming that the rent and other services it pays for the flat are tax-deductible. We then calculate the amount of income tax you must pay for having the use of the flat.

We have used the following assumptions:

The flat is let on a short lease by the company so rent and other associated expenses are paid directly by it. You pay no rent for the use of the flat.

Rent and related expenses paid by the company	£10,000
Corporation Tax rate paid by company	19%
Employers' NI rate	12.8%
Your highest personal tax rate	40%

COMPANY'S TAX POSITION			
	£	£	CT PAYABLE
TAXABLE PROFIT IN COMPANY BEFORE PAYMENT FOR FLAT PROVIDED TO YOU		70,000.00	13,300.00
RENT AND RELATED EXPENSES PAID	10,000.00		
EMPLOYER'S NI ON THE CASH EQUIVALENT VALUE *(12.8% ON £10,000)*	1,280.00		
TOTAL ACCOMMODATION COSTS		-11,280.00	
NET PROFIT AFTER ACCOMMODATION EXPENSES		58,720.00	11,156.80
CT SAVED BY PROVIDING FLAT	-2,143.20		-2,143.20
NET COST TO THE COMPANY *(COSTS LESS CT SAVED)*	9,136.80		

NET COST AS A PERCENTAGE OF RENT AND EXPENSES PAID	91.37%

YOUR TAX POSITION			
EACH TAX YEAR	£	£	%
VALUE OF ACCOMMODATION TO YOU		10,000.00	100%
CASH EQUIVALENT VALUE OF ACCOMMODATION	10,000.00		
INCOME TAX AT 40% *(ON £10,000)*		4,000.00	40%
NET INCREASE IN YOUR POSITION		6,000.00	60%

FREE ACCOMMODATION

SECTION 6: PROS AND CONS

ADVANTAGES OF FREE ACCOMMODATION

1. No employees' NI. You do not have to pay employees' NI on the cash equivalent of the accommodation provided by the company.

2. Cheap option. The company may find that it makes commercial sense to rent or buy a flat for your use whilst you are away on business. If this property is only used by you when away from your normal place of work, and is not used by your family, no tax charge arises.

3. Family use. If you are taxed on the cash equivalent value of the accommodation the tax charge is not increased if your family also use it.

4. Ownership spread. There is a legal limit on the number of people who can be included on the deeds of a property situated in the UK. If the company "owns" the property the ownership is effectively spread between all the shareholders of the company. In other words it's a way around the restriction.

DISADVANTAGES OF FREE ACCOMMODATION

1. The calculation. The cash equivalent value can be time consuming to research and calculate.

2. Employers' NI. The company must pay employers' NI on the annual cash equivalent value of providing the accommodation.

3. Directors. When a director has a material interest in a company the only basis for having tax-free accommodation provided by that company is when their life is in danger.

4. Additional charge. Where the company pays for the services connected to the property that a tenant would normally pay such as electricity, you will taxed on the costs of those services.

5. Taper relief. If the company owns a domestic property that's only used to provide living accommodation for employees, that property may be seen as an investment rather than a working asset of the business. If the value of the investment is significant compared to the other assets the company owns, the Capital Gains Tax discount (known as taper relief) available when the company's shares are sold could be reduced from a maximum of 75% after two years to a maximum of 60% after ten years.

FREE ACCOMMODATION

© PROFIT EXTRACTION, indicator

Profit Extraction

PART 12

Childcare

SECTION 1: METHOD

WHAT IS MEANT BY THE PROVISION OF CHILDCARE?

Paying for childcare can use up a large proportion of your salary, so if your company can bear that cost you will be better off. There are two tax-efficient ways for the company to do this.

Childcare vouchers. A childcare voucher has a face value of a certain monetary amount which can be redeemed against the cost of places for children under 16, in approved nurseries or with registered child minders who participate in the voucher scheme.

Workplace nursery. A workplace nursery is the provision of supervised childcare on premises made available by the company. Such provision is tax- & NI-free.

HOW SHOULD THE CHILDCARE BE PROVIDED?

Childcare vouchers. The vouchers are usually provided by specialist agencies that charge a handling or administration fee of up to 8% of the face value of the voucher. If you buy the childcare voucher personally and the company then reimburses the cost, both you and the company must pay NI on this amount. The childcare vouchers must not be exchangeable for cash. If they are, NI is again payable.

Workplace nursery. This can be either in the same building that the company occupies or in another building hired or acquired for the purpose. The requirements of a workplace nursery may also be met if the company helps to run a commercial nursery. Where the company merely pays for places in a commercial nursery the childcare provision will not count as a workplace nursery, and it will be taxable.

IS THERE A LIMIT TO WHAT THE COMPANY CAN PAY FOR?

Childcare vouchers. There is no upper limit on the value of childcare vouchers you can provide.

Workplace nursery. The company can only provide tax-free childcare for the children who normally live with you, or your own children that you maintain financially. The company cannot provide free childcare for e.g. your grandchildren or nieces and nephews, unless you are financially responsible for them.

© PROFIT EXTRACTION, Indicator

CHILDCARE

SECTION 2: YOUR COMPANY

IS THIS TAX-DEDUCTIBLE FOR THE COMPANY?

Vouchers. The company can deduct the cost of the childcare vouchers it provides to directors and employees.

Nursery. The cost of providing a workplace nursery is completely tax-deductible for the company as long as the nursery is used to provide childcare for the children of the directors and employees.

WHAT IS THE NI COST?

None. There is no employers' NI cost to the company of providing childcare. For the first £50 per week of childcare vouchers there is also no NI cost. However, above £50 a week the company will pay 12.8% on the excess.

WHAT DOES THE COMPANY HAVE TO TELL THE TAXMAN?

P11D. The cost of childcare vouchers (over £50 per week per employee) is taxable, so the full cost to the company (including any handling fee charged by an agency) must be reported.

DOES IT MATTER HOW MUCH THE COMPANY SPENDS?

No. The whole cost of childcare provided by the company is tax-deductible.

However, if the cost of childcare provided is so great as to eliminate the profits of the company, the Taxman may argue that the expenses are not incurred wholly and exclusively for the purposes of the business. In this rare situation the Taxman will not allow the childcare costs to be deducted from the company's profits.

CHILDCARE

SECTION 3: YOU

SHOULD CHILDCARE BE SHOWN ON YOUR TAX RETURN?

Childcare vouchers in excess of £50 per week are a taxable benefit so their cost should be reported on your tax return.

P11D info. The cash equivalent value of the voucher must be included on the "Employment" pages of your tax return under the heading "Benefits and expenses". The figure is the full cost of the voucher to the company, which is the face value of the voucher plus any administration or handling fee paid by the company. The company should report this figure on your P11D, and provide you with the relevant details by July 6 each year.

A workplace nursery is tax-free, as long as it meets the strict legal requirements. So you're not required to report the provision of these childcare places in the nursery on your tax return.

CAN YOU DEDUCT ANY EXPENSES FROM THIS?

No. You cannot deduct expenses from the cash equivalent value of the vouchers.

WHAT IS THE NI COST?

None. Childcare vouchers up to £50 per week are free of employees' NI and childcare provided through a workplace nursery is free of income tax and NI.

AT WHAT RATE WILL THE PROVISION OF CHILDCARE FINALLY BE TAXED?

Childcare vouchers in excess of the £50 tax and NI-free limit are taxable as part of your total income, so the rate of tax applied to the cash equivalent value will be the highest rate that applies to your income in a tax year.

The provision of childcare through a workplace nursery is tax-free.

IS ANY TAX PAYABLE UPFRONT?

PAYE. The taxable cash equivalent value of childcare vouchers your receive from your company is reported to the Taxman on Form P11D. The Taxman should adjust your Pay-As-You-Earn coding to take account of the value of the vouchers received in the previous year. So if you receive the same value of vouchers each year the income tax due should be deducted in advance through the PAYE system.

© PROFIT EXTRACTION, Indicator

SECTION 4: VAT

ARE THERE ANY CONSEQUENCES FOR VAT?

None. There are no VAT consequences of you receiving free childcare vouchers or "free" childcare in a workplace nursery.

© PROFIT EXTRACTION, Indicator

SECTION 5: EXAMPLE

This is an example of the tax-related consequences of the company providing you with childcare vouchers.

We first look at what the provision of childcare vouchers costs your company in net terms. We are taking into account the fact that the vouchers are tax-deductible for the company. We will then calculate the net amount that you will be left with as an individual after deduction of income tax.

We have used the following assumptions:

Face value of childcare vouchers	£5,000
Administration fee paid by company (8%)	£400
Corporation Tax (CT) rate paid by company	19%
Your highest personal tax rate	40%
£50 per week tax and NI-free limit	£2,600 p.a.

COMPANY'S TAX POSITION			
	£	£	CT PAYABLE
TAXABLE PROFIT IN COMPANY BEFORE CHILDCARE VOUCHERS		70,000.00	13,300.00
TOTAL COST OF CHILDCARE VOUCHERS (FACE VALUE PLUS ADMIN FEE)	5,400.00		
EMPLOYERS NI (£5,400 - £2,600) AT 12.8%	358.40	-5,758.40	
NET PROFIT AFTER COST OF VOUCHERS		64,241.60	12,205.90
CT SAVED BY PROVIDING CHILDCARE VOUCHERS	-1,094.10		-1,094.10
NET COST TO THE COMPANY (COST LESS CT SAVED)	4,664.30		

NET COST AS A PERCENTAGE		86.37%	
YOUR TAX POSITION			
	£	£	%
VALUE TO YOU OF CHILDCARE VOUCHERS (I.E. FACE VALUE)		5,000.00	100.00%
TAXABLE BENEFIT OF CHILDCARE VOUCHERS (£5,400 - £2,600)	2,800.00		
INCOME TAX DUE AT 40% (ON £2,800)	-1,120.00		
EMPLOYEE'S NI (£5,400 - £2,600) AT 1%	-28.00	-1,148.00	22.96%
NET INCREASE IN YOUR POSITION		3,852.00	77.04%

© PROFIT EXTRACTION, Indicator

SECTION 6: PROS & CONS

ADVANTAGES OF COMPANY-PROVIDED CHILDCARE

1. Cost saving. Childcare vouchers can save you many thousands of pounds a year in childminder fees.

2. Tax-free nursery. Your company can provide tax-free childcare for your children and those of your employees by setting up a workplace nursery.

3. NI savings. The first £50 per week of childcare vouchers are free of both employees' and employers' NI and income tax when they are purchased directly by the company.

4. Reduces Corporation Tax. The cost of providing childcare vouchers or a workplace nursery is completely tax-deductible for the company, and so will reduce the Corporation Tax it pays.

5. Per parent. The £50 limit is per parent rather than per child. So if your spouse works in the company as well as you, you can extract £100 per week tax-free.

DISADVANTAGES OF COMPANY-PROVIDED CHILDCARE

1. Workplace Nursery. The company must be involved in the management and running of the workplace nursery for it to be tax-free for employees. It must be registered with the local authority and therefore be subject to inspections. The nursery cannot be operated on domestic premises.

2. Vouchers are not completely tax-free. The cost of childcare vouchers in excess of £50 is taxable in the hands of the recipients.

3. Reimbursements. If the company reimburses you for the cost of childcare, or for childcare vouchers you have purchased, those costs are taxable and subject to NI.

4. Open to all. You will have to open the scheme up to all employees. Although this shouldn't be a major problem as the company will be saving 12.8% on the first £50 per employee.

5. Loss of tax credits. If you currently receive tax credits, then you may be worse off by taking vouchers rather than, say, increased salary.

Profit Extraction

Medical expenses

SECTION 1: METHOD

WHAT IS MEANT BY MEDICAL EXPENSES?

A number of different scenarios arise under this heading. There is your company paying for the cost of medical treatment itself or alternatively the premiums on an insurance policy to cover such costs. As a separate issue, it can also pay for periodic medical check-ups for both you and your family.

Trips abroad. Any medical expenses incurred while you are working abroad for the company are tax-free if the company pays them on your behalf. The same applies to any insurance for such expenses.

HOW SHOULD YOU WITHDRAW THE COST OF MEDICAL EXPENSES?

Insurance. Private health insurance for medical treatment in the UK is taxable, whether you pay for the insurance and the company reimburses the cost, or the company pays for the insurance directly. However, the company may be able to negotiate a discount if it buys medical insurance for a number of its employees, directors and their families covered by one policy.

If you take out a medical insurance policy in your own name and the company pays the premiums for you, there will also be an NI cost as the company has paid a liability on your behalf.

Other medical expenses. These may be only partially tax-free. For example, paying for a routine medical examination is tax-free but any treatments that result from it are taxable and will attract NI if paid for by the company. To avoid the company paying for treatments that involve an extra NI charge, it can arrange to pay for the medical examination directly and provide you with a voucher to redeem against the total medical bill.

Eye tests. If you need to use Display Screen Equipment (DSE) for your work the company can pay for a regular eye test and for any spectacles you need solely to use that DSE safely, completely tax-free. If only part of your requirement for glasses relates to DSE work, only that part will be tax-free if paid for by the company. It is important that you get an itemised receipt from the optician that details the cost of the eye test and the components of the spectacle cost if the company is to reimburse the expense.

IS THERE A MAXIMUM THAT CAN BE SPENT THIS WAY?

Generally no. Tax law does not limit how much can be spent on medical expenses.

SECTION 2: YOUR COMPANY

ARE MEDICAL EXPENSES TAX-DEDUCTIBLE?

Yes. All medical expenses the company pays on behalf of its employees and directors are tax-deductible.

WHAT IS THE NI COST?

The cost of a group medical insurance policy, arranged by the company to cover a number of employees, attracts employers' NI at 12.8%. This is payable by the company by July 6 following the end of the tax year (April 5).

IS IT IMPORTANT HOW MUCH THE COMPANY SPENDS?

Yes. As the company can deduct the medical expenses from its profits before the calculation of Corporation Tax, they can reduce the tax paid.

Exception. The Taxman can argue that excessive medical costs borne on behalf of a director who controls the company are in reality a "private expense" of that director. In these rare cases the Taxman will not allow the company to claim a tax deduction without some negotiation taking place.

MEDICAL EXPENSES

SECTION 3: YOU

SHOULD THE MEDICAL EXPENSES BE SHOWN ON YOUR TAX RETURN?

Yes. You must include the taxable value of the medical expenses on the "Employment" pages on your tax return.

The taxable value of medical expenses should be shown on the P11D the company prepares for every director and higher paid employee (more than £8,500 pa). The company must provide you with a copy of the information included on Form P11D by July 6 after the end of the tax year. Of course tax-free medical expenses (such as check-ups) do not have to be reported on your tax return.

CAN YOU DEDUCT ANY EXPENSES FROM THIS BENEFIT-IN-KIND?

No. There are no expenses that can be deducted.

WHAT IS THE NI COST?

None. If you are a member of a group insurance scheme paid for by the company there is no employees' NI cost to you.

The cost of eye tests and glasses needed to help you to use DSE as part of your work is always free of NI. Similarly the cost of medical treatment required while working abroad is NI-free.

Arranged yourself. The cost of an individual medical insurance policy, which you arrange, but is either paid by the company or the company reimburses you for, attracts NI for both you and the company.

AT WHAT RATE WILL MEDICAL EXPENSES FINALLY BE TAXED?

Taxable medical expenses are treated as if they were part of your salary, so the rate of tax applied will be the highest that applies to your salary.

WHEN WILL YOU BE TAXED ON MEDICAL EXPENSES?

When the medical expenses are taxable, their value should be reported on Form P11D each tax year.

Tax code altered. If the company pays the same amount of taxable medical expenses on your behalf each year, the Taxman will include that amount in your Pay-As-You-Earn code. The operation of that code will allow (approximately) the right amount of tax to be deducted from your monthly salary.

MEDICAL EXPENSES

© PROFIT EXTRACTION, Indicator

SECTION 4: VAT

ARE THERE ANY CONSEQUENCES FOR VAT?

None. There are no VAT consequences of having your medical expenses paid by your company.

MEDICAL EXPENSES

SECTION 5: EXAMPLE

This is an example of the tax-related consequences of the company paying an insurance premium on your behalf.

We first look at what the medical insurance costs are to your company in net terms. We are taking into account the fact that the medical expense is tax-deductible for the company. We will then calculate the net amount that you will be left with as an individual after deduction of income tax.

We have used the following assumptions:

Cost of medical insurance to the company	£4,000
Corporation Tax (CT) rate paid by company	19%
Employers' NI payable by the company	12.8%
Your highest personal tax rate	40%

COMPANY'S TAX POSITION			
	£	**£**	**CT PAYABLE**
TAXABLE PROFIT IN COMPANY BEFORE MEDICAL INSURANCE		70,000.00	13,300.00
COST OF MEDICAL INSURANCE COVER THROUGH GROUP POLICY	4,000.00		
EMPLOYERS' NI ON MEDICAL INSURANCE COST (12.8% x £4,000)	512.00		
TOTAL COST OF MEDICAL INSURANCE		-4,512.00	
NET PROFIT AFTER COST OF INSURANCE		65,488.00	12,442.72
CT SAVED BY PROVIDING MEDICAL INSURANCE	-857.28		-857.28
NET COST TO THE COMPANY (COSTS LESS CT SAVED)	3,654.72		

NET COST AS A PERCENTAGE	91.37%

YOUR TAX POSITION		
	£	**%**
TAXABLE BENEFIT-IN-KIND	4,000.00	100%
INCOME TAX DUE AT 40% (ON £4,000)	-1,600.00	40%
NET VALUE OF MEDICAL INSURANCE PROVIDED	2,400.00	60%

© PROFIT EXTRACTION, Indicator

MEDICAL EXPENSES

SECTION 6: PROS & CONS

ADVANTAGES OF THE COMPANY PAYING MEDICAL EXPENSES

1. Group policies. You can achieve a cost saving by the company paying for medical insurance on a group basis.

2. Health checks. The company can pay for routine health checks for you and your family completely free of tax and NI.

3. Eye tests. If you need to use DSE as part of your job, (and most people do) the company can pay for a regular eye test and the cost of the prescription that relates to using the DSE. You do not have to pay tax or NI on these costs.

4. Overseas cover. When you are required to work overseas the company can pay for medical insurance and any medical treatment you need with no tax or NI charges arising.

5. Tax-deductible. The medical expenses paid by the company are completely tax-deductible and can reduce the amount of Corporation Tax it pays.

DISADVANTAGES OF THE COMPANY PAYING MEDICAL EXPENSES

1. Employers' NI. The cost of medical treatment (other than when working abroad), and insurance for that treatment is taxable and subject to an employers' NI charge.

2. Spectacles. The prescription for your spectacle lenses must relate to your work using DSE. The tax exemption will not cover the cost of the glasses you need e.g. for driving or other distance viewing.

MEDICAL EXPENSES

Profit Extraction

Family dividend

SECTION 1: METHOD

WHAT IS A FAMILY DIVIDEND?

When members of your family own shares in your company they can receive dividends paid in respect of those shares, as a so-called family dividend. A dividend is paid for a particular type and class of share, at the same number of pence per share to each shareholder who holds shares of that class.

Income can be diverted from you to other members of your family by sharing the dividend. The family member may well pay less tax on the dividend than you.

HOW DO YOU SET UP A FAMILY DIVIDEND?

Shares. Before your family members can receive dividends from the company they must acquire shares in it, either as a gift or by purchasing them from other shareholders or from the company itself.

Gifting shares. If you give shares which are registered in your name to your spouse or immediate family, the Taxman may argue that you are creating what is known as a settlement, under which you will ultimately benefit because your gift of shares will reduce your income in favour of your child or spouse. In these circumstances the Taxman will pretend the gift has not happened and tax you on all the dividends issued in respect of the shares you formerly held.

Purchase. The Taxman has less to argue about if the family members buy their shares directly from the company in what is known as a subscription. Ideally the family member should use his or her own money to subscribe for the shares.

Children. A child aged under 18 can legally hold shares in his or her own name. However, the child may not have his own money to subscribe for the shares. If the child is very young it's good practice for a trust to be formed to acquire and hold the shares on his or her behalf. Someone other than the child's parents should provide the trust funds. If the parent provides the trust fund, the dividends that are paid into the trust will be taxed on the parent and not on the child. Professional advice should always be sought before using a trust.

Waiver. If all the shareholders hold the same class of shares you can sign a declaration not to receive (waive) the dividend due to you. The total dividend then gets shared out amongst the other shareholders. To do this you must submit your waiver letter for the dividend to the company before the shareholders approve it. You cannot waive a dividend after you obtain the right to receive it.

Flexible dividends. Alternatively, a company may issue different types of shares, such as Class B Ordinary shares or Preference shares to your family. Income can then be diverted from you to other members of your family because a dividend can be paid only for the particular type and class of shares held by them and not you (see Part 18).

Payment. The dividend may be paid in cash, by cheque or electronic transfer into the shareholder's bank account. If the recipient of the dividend is a child who does not have a bank or savings account in his or her name, the dividend should be paid into an account held by an adult as nominee for the child. Where your spouse holds shares in the company, the dividend should be paid into an account held in his or her

© PROFIT EXTRACTION, Indicator

sole name rather than an account in your joint names. If the dividend is paid into a savings account in your joint names the Taxman may argue that it has been paid to you rather than your spouse, and may seek to tax you on it.

SECTION 2: YOUR COMPANY

IS THE FAMILY DIVIDEND TAX-DEDUCTIBLE FOR THE COMPANY?

No. Dividends are not tax-deductible for the company whoever they are paid to. The dividend is paid out of the company's profits after tax has been charged on them.

WHAT IS THE NI COST?

None. There is no employers' NI on family dividends.

SHOULD THE COMPANY DEDUCT TAX WHEN PAYING THE FAMILY DIVIDEND?

No. The company should not deduct tax or NI when it pays a dividend.

Tax credit. The shareholder receives the net value of the dividend as paid by the company plus a notional tax credit of one ninth of the net value. This tax credit is not real money; the Taxman cannot pay it out to the shareholder and it has nothing to do with the amount of Corporation Tax paid by the company. The tax credit is just a useful device to ensure that shareholders who are taxed at the lower or basic rate of tax (10% or 22%) have no more tax to pay on their dividend.

ANY RESTRICTIONS ON PAYING A DIVIDEND?

Yes. The shareholders must be paid dividends in proportion to the number of shares they hold.

Example.

The company has retained profits of £12,000 to pay out as a dividend. It has five shareholders who own the following shares:

ALFIE	CATHY	BROOKLYN	DAVID	ELSIE	TOTAL SHARES
20	10	10	10	10	60

The dividend must be distributed as follows:

ALFIE	CATHY	BROOKLYN	DAVID	ELSIE	TOTAL DIVIDEND
£4,000	£2,000	£2,000	£2,000	£2,000	£12,000

Profits needed. If a company has profits it can pay a dividend to its shareholders. If the directors allow a dividend to be paid at a time when there are not enough retained profits to cover that payment, the dividend will be illegal. In this case the Taxman may treat the dividend payment as a loan to the shareholders which can create a further tax charge, (see Part 6).

© PROFIT EXTRACTION, Indicator

SECTION 3: YOU

SHOULD THE FAMILY DIVIDEND BE SHOWN ON YOUR TAX RETURN?

No. The family dividend must be shown on the tax return of the individual shareholder who received the dividend. If a family member has income of less than £37,295 (£32,400 + £4,895) in the 2005/06 tax year (including the tax credit attached to the dividend), he or she should not have to complete a tax return as there is no further tax to pay in respect of the dividends received.

CAN YOU DEDUCT ANY EXPENSES FROM THE FAMILY DIVIDEND?

No. There are no expenses that can be deducted from dividend income.

Allowances. If the family member has no other income in the tax year, his or her tax-free personal allowance is set against the dividend income, which reduces the total amount of taxable income for the tax year.

WHAT IS THE NI COST?

None. There is no employees' NI payable on family dividends.

AT WHAT RATE WILL THE FAMILY DIVIDEND FINALLY BE TAXED?

It depends. The tax rate applied to dividend income depends on the level of other taxable income received by the shareholder in the same tax year. The income tax rates that apply to dividends received in 2005/06 are:

FAMILY DIVIDEND TAX RATES	
TAXABLE INCOME	**TAX RATE**
FIRST £32,400	10%
ABOVE £32,400	32.5%

If the shareholder is a 22% taxpayer (taxable income below £32,400 for 2005/06) they will have no further tax to pay on the dividend income.

FAMILY DIVIDEND

SECTION 4: VAT

ARE THERE ANY CONSEQUENCES FOR VAT?

None. Withdrawing a dividend from a company has no VAT consequences.

© PROFIT EXTRACTION, indicator

FAMILY DIVIDEND

SECTION 5: EXAMPLE

This is an example of the tax-related consequences of paying a dividend to a member of your family instead of to you.

We first look at what the company must pay in Corporation Tax to have net profits available to pay the dividend. We then calculate the net amount that you and your spouse (or other family member) will be left with as individuals after deduction of income tax. This computation should be compared to Example 2 in Part 3 where the full £50,000 dividend was paid to you alone.

We have used the following assumptions:

Total taxable profit made by the company	£70,000
Total dividend approved	£50,000
Paid to you	£40,000
Paid to your spouse	£10,000
Corporation Tax (CT) rate paid by the company	19%
Your highest income tax rate payable on a dividend	32.5%
Your spouse's highest tax rate payable on a dividend	10%
Tax credit on dividend	1/9

COMPANY'S TAX POSITION		
	£	
AFTER-TAX PROFITS NEEDED TO PAY THE DIVIDEND	50,000.00	100.00%
CT PAYABLE TO ARRIVE AT THESE PROFITS ((£50,000/ 81) x 19)	11,728.40	
THEREFORE THE COMPANY HAS TO MAKE PROFITS BEFORE TAX OF ((£50,000 / 81) x 100)	61,728.40	123.45%

YOUR TAX POSITION				
	You (£)	Your spouse (£)	Total	%
DIVIDEND PAID	40,000.00	10,000.00	50,000.00	100.00%
TAX CREDIT ON DIVIDEND (1/9 x DIVIDEND PAID)	4,444.44	1,111.11		
GROSS TAXABLE DIVIDEND (DIVIDEND PLUS TAX CREDIT)	44,444.44	11,111.11		
LESS PERSONAL ALLOWANCE	-	-4,895.00		
TAXABLE INCOME	44,444.44	6,216.11		
INCOME TAX AT 10%	-	-621.61		
INCOME TAX AT 32.5%	-14,444.44	-		
TAX CREDIT SET AGAINST TAX ON DIVIDEND (RESTRICTED TO TAX CHARGED)	4,444.44	621.61		
TOTAL TAXES	10,000.00	-	10,000.00	20%
NET DIVIDEND AVAILABLE TO SPEND (DIVIDEND PAID LESS TOTAL TAXES)	30,000.00	10,000.00	40,000.00	80%

FAMILY DIVIDEND

SECTION 6: PROS & CONS

ADVANTAGES OF PAYING A FAMILY DIVIDEND

1. NI saving. The company does not have to pay employers' NI on the dividend payment and the recipient of the dividend pays no employees' NI on that income.

2. Less income tax. Income can be diverted from you to other members of your family by the company issuing dividends. The family member may well pay less tax on the dividend than you would if you received the same dividend in addition to your other income from the company.

3. No duties. The family member does not have to work for the company to receive a dividend.

4. Children. There are no legal restrictions on children receiving dividend payments from the company, as long as the shares are registered in the child's name or in the name of a nominee who holds the shares on their behalf.

5. Flexible. The amount of the dividend payment can be varied to suit the amount of profits available in the company, unlike a salary that must be paid at a similar level each month.

6. Different shares. Family members can hold different classes of shares that entitle them to different rates of dividend payments (see Part 18). These various dividend rates can be used to reward individual family members in the most tax-efficient manner according to each person's marginal tax rate.

DISADVANTAGES OF PAYING A FAMILY DIVIDEND

1. Tax credit. The tax credit on a dividend paid to a family member who has no other income, will be partially wasted where income is covered by that individual's tax-free personal allowance.

2. One class. Where there is only one class of share, the company must pay dividends at the same rate to all shareholders who have not waived their entitlement to the dividend in advance.

3. Share value. Regular dividend payments will increase the value of the small number of shares held by family members. This can have implications for Capital Gains Tax.

4. Dilute holding. Each family member that receives a dividend from the company must hold a share in the company. This distribution of shares will dilute your holding and may reduce your control over the affairs of the company.

5. Settlement. If you give shares in your company to your immediate family members, such as your spouse and children, the Taxman can argue that the gift was made to allow you to divert some of your income to these individuals. The Taxman may then insist that any dividends paid on the shares you gave away should be taxed on you rather than the recipients of those dividends, so your tax saving is lost.

FAMILY DIVIDEND

© PROFIT EXTRACTION, indicator

Profit Extraction

Family salary

SECTION 1: METHOD

WHAT IS MEANT BY FAMILY SALARY?

The company can pay a salary to a member of your family who works for it.

It's possible to reduce your own salary and pay a little bit more to the family member to reduce the total amount of income tax and NI that the family as a whole pays. This tax saving is explored in the Example section.

HOW SHOULD YOU WITHDRAW FAMILY SALARY?

The family member should be paid through the payroll just like any other employee. First, your company takes off any income tax and NI due and then pays the balance (the net amount) over to the family member either in the form of cash, cheque or electronic transfer to their bank account.

Make sure it's paid. The Taxman is sometimes suspicious when a company employs family members of a director. He thinks you may be hiding part of your earnings by paying them out in the name of your spouse or child. If the Taxman can show that the family member's salary has been paid to you rather than the individual named, you will be taxed on this amount in addition to your own salary. If your spouse works for the company it's easier to show that he or she has actually received a salary if it's paid into a bank account in their own name, rather than into a bank account held in your joint names.

HOW MUCH CAN YOU ACTUALLY PAY?

Adults. The company must pay at least the National Minimum Wage (NMW) to any family member aged over 16 who works for the company. This is a minimum hourly rate that is set by law and monitored by the Taxman. The NMW rates that apply are:

NATIONAL MINIMUM WAGE RATES		
Age of worker	**Current rate**	**Rate from Oct 1, 2005**
16-17	£3.00 PER HOUR	£3.00 PER HOUR
18-21	£4.10 PER HOUR	£4.25 PER HOUR
22 AND OVER	£4.85 PER HOUR	£5.05 PER HOUR

Children. The company must observe the strict rules and regulations for employing children aged under 16. These rules are monitored by the Local Education Authority and limit the number of hours a child can work. Children under the age of 13 cannot be employed except for light duties in very limited circumstances. It is illegal to employ a child in a factory.

© PROFIT EXTRACTION, Indicator

SECTION 2: YOUR COMPANY

IS THE FAMILY SALARY TAX-DEDUCTIBLE FOR THE COMPANY?

Yes. A salary paid to a genuine employee of the company will always be tax-deductible for the company.

Exception. The Taxman will often look at the level of salary paid to family members of the company directors. He will want to know whether the amount paid is at or above the market rate for the job. If the pay is excessive the Taxman can argue that the reward does not reflect the work done so the payment is not wholly and exclusively made for the company's trade. So some negotiation may be required with the Taxman to settle on an amount that is deductible.

SHOULD THE COMPANY DEDUCT TAX WHEN PAYING A SALARY TO A FAMILY MEMBER?

Yes. As with any employee, the company must deduct income tax and NI under the Pay-As-You-Earn (PAYE) scheme.

Students. If the family member has taken out a student loan (since August 1999) the company may have to deduct an amount from his or her salary as a repayment of that loan. The Taxman will tell the company whether it must make student loan deductions from the individual's salary, and provide a table to help work out the amount due. If the family member's salary is less than £10,000 per year no student loan deductions are required. The Taxman collects the student loan repayments on behalf of the Student Loan Company, so all student loan deductions should be paid over to him along with the total tax and NI amounts deducted from the entire payroll.

WHAT IS THE NI COST?

The company has to pay employers' NI on each salary, at the following rates:

EMPLOYERS' NI RATES	
Annual salary	**2005/06**
UP TO £4,895 (OR £94 A WEEK)	0%
AMOUNTS OVER £4,895 (OR £94 A WEEK)	12.8%

DOES IT MATTER HOW MUCH FAMILY SALARY IS PAID?

Yes. The salary the company pays reduces its taxable profits which in turn reduces the Corporation Tax (CT) it suffers. However, if the company exists to hold investments rather than carry on a trade it must pay CT at 30%, whatever the level of its taxable profits.

IR35. If your company provides your personal services to other businesses it may be caught by the tax rules known as IR35. If this is the case most of the company's income must be withdrawn as salary by you as the main worker. You should seek professional advice here.

FAMILY SALARY

SECTION 3: YOU

SHOULD THE FAMILY SALARY BE SHOWN ON YOUR TAX RETURN?

No. The salary paid to a family member should be shown on that individual's tax return form, not on your own. The family member may not be required to complete a tax return form if their salary is taxed at the basic or lower rate of income tax and they have no other untaxed income.

CAN ANY EXPENSES BE DEDUCTED FROM THE FAMILY SALARY?

Limited. The family member may be able to deduct some limited expenses in the form of mileage allowances for a private car used for business journeys, professional subscriptions to approved bodies, or a flat-rate allowance for small tools or protective clothing required for the job (see Part 1).

WHAT IS THE NI COST?

None to you. Your earnings are ignored when calculating the employees' NI due on their salary.

NI saving. For each employment a family member starts with the same annual NI-free amount £4,895 (£94 a week). Therefore £4,895 of income that would otherwise be subject to NI as part of your salary is NI-free if paid to them instead.

The rates of employees' NI that apply for 2005/06 are as follows:

EMPLOYEES' NI RATES	
ANNUAL SALARY	**2005/06**
FIRST £4,895 (OR £94 PER WEEK)	0%
NEXT £27,865	11%
AMOUNTS OVER £32,760 (OR £630 PER WEEK)	1%

AT WHAT RATE WILL FAMILY SALARY FINALLY BE TAXED?

It depends. The rate of tax that the family member must pay on his or her salary from the company depends on the level of his or her total income for the tax year. If this rate is less than yours, then diverting salary to them will produce income tax savings. The income tax rates on total taxable income for 2005/06 are: 10% on the first £2,090, 22% on the next £30,310 and 40% above £32,400.

© PROFIT EXTRACTION, Indicator

FAMILY SALARY

SECTION 4: VAT

ARE THERE ANY CONSEQUENCES FOR VAT?

No. Withdrawing a salary from your company has no VAT consequences. Pay and salaries are not subject to VAT.

© PROFIT EXTRACTION, indicator

SECTION 5: EXAMPLE

This is an example of the tax-related consequences of your company paying a salary to a member of your family instead of to you.

We first look at what the payment of the salaries costs your company. We will then calculate the net amount that you and your spouse will be left with after the deduction of income tax and NI charges.

We have used the following assumptions:

Increase in salary	£15,000
Salary for you	£7,500
Salary for your spouse	£7,500
Corporation Tax (CT) rate paid by the company	19%
Your highest personal tax rate	40%
Employers' NI rate	12.8%
Employees' NI rate	11% and 1%

COMPANY'S TAX POSITION			
2005/06	**£**	**£**	**CT PAYABLE**
TAXABLE PROFIT IN THE COMPANY BEFORE INCREASE IN SALARIES		70,000.00	13,300.00
INCREASE IN SALARIES	15,000.00		
EMPLOYERS' NI *(12.8% x £15,000)*	1,920.00		
TOTAL SALARY COSTS		-16,920.00	
NET PROFIT AFTER SALARY INCREASES		53,080.00	10,085.20
CT SAVED BY PAYING SALARIES	-3,214.80		-3,214.80
NET COST FOR COMPANY *(COSTS LESS CT SAVED)*	13,705.20		

NET COST AS A PERCENTAGE	91.37%

YOUR TAX POSITION				
2005/06	**YOU (£)**	**YOUR SPOUSE (£)**	**TOTAL (£)**	**%**
GROSS SALARY	7,500.00	7,500.00	15,000.00	100%
EMPLOYEES' NI*	-75.00	-825.00		
INCOME TAX AT 22%	-	-1,650.00		
INCOME TAX AT 40%	-3,000.00	-		
TOTAL TAXES	-3,075.00	-2,475.00	5,550.00	37%
NET SALARY AVAILABLE TO SPEND *(GROSS SALARY - TOTAL TAXES)*	4,425.00	5,025.00	9,450.00	63%

__Employees' NI.__ As a 40% taxpayer you would pay a further 1% NI on this increase in salary.

FAMILY SALARY

© PROFIT EXTRACTION, indicator

SECTION 6: PROS & CONS

ADVANTAGES OF A FAMILY SALARY

1. Lower income tax. A salary paid to a family member may be taxed at a lower rate than it would be if it were paid as part of your salary.

2. NI savings. A salary £94 per week or less paid to a family member is free of NI.

3. Tax-deductible. Reasonable salaries paid to family members are tax-deductible for the company, and can reduce the level of Corporation Tax paid by it.

DISADVANTAGES OF A FAMILY SALARY

1. Real work. The family member must perform some real work for the company to justify the reward of a salary.

2. Minimum wage. The company must pay an adult family member an amount that is at least equal to the National Minimum Wage for the hours worked.

3. Co-operation. The family members must be willing to cooperate with you to achieve the tax savings described above.

Profit Extraction

PART 16

Selling to the company

SECTION 1: METHOD

WHAT IS MEANT BY SELLING TO THE COMPANY?

As an individual you can sell an asset such as a building, a vehicle or other goods that you own to the company.

HOW SHOULD YOU WITHDRAW THE SALE PROCEEDS?

Invoice. When you sell goods or services to the company you should issue an invoice showing the total value of the items or services provided and the VAT due (if any). You can stipulate the terms of payment on the invoice. If the company delays payment beyond the period stated in your terms you can charge interest on the overdue amount.

Capital. When you sell a large capital asset such as a building to the company, the terms of payment will be included within the contract of sale drawn up by your solicitor.

Leave it in. It's possible to leave the amount owing to you for the sale of an asset to the company as a loan from you. The company should credit the amount owing to your director's loan account, and you will be able to draw the money owed when the cash is available. The company can also pay you interest on the outstanding purchase price (see Part 4).

DOES IT MATTER WHAT PRICE YOU CHARGE?

Goods. The profit you make on selling things to the company will be taxed in your hands as your income, so the greater the proceeds, the more profit you are likely to make and the more tax you will have to pay.

Assets. When you sell an asset to your company such as a building, the profit you make, will be subject to Capital Gains Tax rather than income tax. The higher the price the company pays for the asset, the greater the gain in your hands and the more tax you will have to pay.

© PROFIT EXTRACTION, Indicator

SECTION 2: YOUR COMPANY

IS THE PAYMENT TAX-DEDUCTIBLE FOR THE COMPANY?

Yes. If you sell goods or services to the company, which it uses as part of its trade, the cost of those items is tax-deductible.

Capital asset. If you sell your interest in a retail property to the company, the cost of it cannot be deducted. The company will only achieve some tax relief on the cost of the property when it sells on its interest in the building in the future.

On a smaller scale, when the company purchases, for example, a car from you, it can set 25% of purchase price (or £3,000 whichever is the lower) each year against its profits.

WHAT IS THE NI COST?

None. There is no employers' NI due on these transactions.

SHOULD THE COMPANY DEDUCT TAX WHEN PAYING YOU?

No. Your company should not deduct tax from the payments it makes to you in satisfaction of your invoices.

DOES IT MATTER HOW MUCH THE COMPANY PAYS YOU?

No. If you own most of the shares in the company so that you control the votes connected with those shares, you and the company are known as connected parties. For tax purposes all transactions between connected parties are deemed to occur at market value even if no money changes hands. You will be taxed on the profit from the sale as if you had received the market value for the asset.

Disclosure in the accounts. As a director of the company you are also known as a related party. All significant transactions with related parties must be shown in a note to the company's annual accounts. This is where the Taxman will pick them up from to ask the market value question.

SELLING TO THE COMPANY

SECTION 3: YOU

SHOULD THE SALES INCOME BE SHOWN ON YOUR TAX RETURN?

Income. Your income from selling goods or services on a regular basis to the company must be reported on the "Self-employment" pages of your tax return. According to the Taxman when you sell goods or services on a regular basis you are carrying on a trade in your own name and must be treated as a self-employed person.

Gains. If you sell a capital asset to the company you must report this on the "Capital Gains" pages of your tax return. However, if all the gains you make total less than £8,500 (for 2005/06), you do not have to report them. You are also saved the bother of making an entry on these pages if the assets are: (1) cars; (2) property you occupied within the last three years as your main home; (3) government stocks known as gilts; (4) foreign currency; and (5) moveable possessions (known as chattels) sold for less than £6,000.

A loss? If, for some reason, you generate a loss when selling an asset to your company it can also be recorded on the "Capital Gains" pages. However, you will only able to set that loss against gains between you and your company, which means you can't offset them against, say, investment gains.

WHAT IS THE NI COST?

Asset sales. When you sell an asset to your company there is no NI charge on the capital gain you make.

Class 2 NI. As a self-employed person you must register with the Taxman to pay Class 2 NI within three months of the date on which you started your trade. This date will normally be the day when you made your first sale.

Payment. You pay a flat rate of £2.10 per week if your self-employed profits are likely to amount to more than £4,345 in the tax year. The Class 2 NI must be paid quarterly or four-weekly by direct debit or in satisfaction of a demand from the Taxman.

Class 4 NI. When you sell goods or services in your own name the profit you make on that trade is subject to an NI charge called Class 4. This is charged at the rate of 8% profits between £4,895 and £32,760, (for 2005/06) and 1% on profits made above £32,760.

Payment. The Class 4 NI must be paid with the income tax due on your self-employed profits i.e. via your tax return.

Maximum NI. If you are employed at the same time as having self-employed income you can apply to defer paying NI. If you earn at least £32,760 as a director of the company you have already paid the maximum amount of NI due for the tax year. You can still apply to defer NI but not the extra 1% NI charge on earnings over £32,760.

SELLING TO THE COMPANY

© PROFIT EXTRACTION, Indicator

CAN YOU DEDUCT ANY EXPENSES FROM THE SALES INCOME?

Trade. If you regularly sell goods or services to the company you will be treated as operating a trade in your own name. Any expenses that are incurred wholly and exclusively for that trade can be deducted from the sales income before you pay tax on the net amount.

Assets. If you sell an asset to the company you can deduct its cost from the sale proceeds to calculate the net gain you are taxed on. Any costs of improvements you have made to that asset may also be deducted. In addition, the cost of professional fees you incur in the transaction, such as conveyancing fees, are also deductible.

AT WHAT RATE WILL THE SALES INCOME FINALLY BE TAXED?

Profits. The rate of tax that applies to the profits you make when you sell items to the company depends on your total income during the tax year. The income tax rates for trading and earned income in tax year 2005/06 are: 10% on the first £2,090, 22% on the next £30,310 and 40% above £32,400.

Gains. If you make a capital gain on selling assets to your company the tax you pay depends on the level of your other income during the tax year and on whether you have any capital losses that can be set against the gain. Currently, the first £8,500 of capital gains made in one tax year are tax-free. The remaining gains are first set against losses made in the same year (or brought forward from earlier years) made on transactions with the same company. The net gains are added to your other income to see what tax band they fall into. The tax rates that apply to gains in 2005/06 are: 20% on up to £32,400 and 40% on any amounts above this.

SECTION 4: VAT

Your company. If you include VAT on your invoice, your company must pay it. If your company is VAT registered it will then be able to claim it back via its VAT return.

You. Whether you are required to charge VAT depends on what is sold and the total value of the invoices you issue. VAT is chargeable once your total sales exceed, or are expected to exceed, the current registration limit of £60,000 (from April 1, 2005). Of course before you issue an invoice that includes VAT you must register with the VATman.

Three years old. You don't have to charge VAT on the sale of a domestic property or sale/lease of a commercial building, if it's more than three years old.

Cars. Even as a VAT registered person you don't charge VAT on the sale of a pre-owned car, provided you sell that car for less than you bought it for.

© PROFIT EXTRACTION, indicator

SECTION 5: EXAMPLE

EXAMPLE 1.

We have used the following assumptions:

You acted as the middleman on the purchase of goods by your company. This is an expense of the company so the full cost is charged against the company's profits in the period the goods are purchased.

Value of goods supplied by you during the year	£12,000
Corporation Tax (CT) rates paid by the company	19%
Your highest personal tax rate	40%
Class 4 NI *(on self-employed income)* between £4,895 and £32,760	8%
Class 2 NI *(on self-employed income)* for the year *(52 weeks x £2.10)*	£109.20

COMPANY'S TAX POSITION			
	£	**£**	**CT PAYABLE**
TAXABLE PROFIT BEFORE PAYMENT FOR THE GOODS		70,000.00	13,300.00
PRICE PAID BY THE COMPANY FOR THE GOODS	12,000.00	-12,000.00	
NET PROFIT AFTER PAYING FOR GOODS		58,000.00	11,020.00
CT SAVED	-2,280.00		-2,280.00
NET COST FOR COMPANY *(COST LESS CT SAVED)*	9,720.00		

NET COST AS A PERCENTAGE	81%

YOUR TAX POSITION			
2005/06	**£**	**£**	**%**
SELF-EMPLOYED INCOME *(IF NO EXPENSES DEDUCTED)*		12,000.00	100.00%
CLASS 4 NI AT 8% *(ON £12,000 - £4,895)*	-568.40		
CLASS 2 NI	-109.20		
INCOME TAX AT 40% *(ON £12,000)*	-4,800.00		
TOTAL TAXES		-5,477.60	45.65%
NET INCOME AVAILABLE TO SPEND		6,522.40	54.35%

SELLING TO THE COMPANY

EXAMPLE 2.

We have used the following assumptions:

You sell your car to the company at its trade-in value of £8,000. The company can charge up to 25% of the cost of the car against its profits in the year of purchase. The balance of the cost must be charged against the company's profits at the rate of 25% of the tax value each year until the car is sold or scrapped.

Market value of the car	£8,000
Corporation Tax (CT) rate paid by company	19%
Your highest tax rate	40%

COMPANY'S TAX POSITION			
	£	£	CT PAYABLE
PROFITS MADE BY THE COMPANY		70,000.00	13,300.00
PRICE PAID FOR THE CAR	8,000.00		
CAPITAL ALLOWANCES AVAILABLE ON THE CAR *(SPREAD OVER SEVERAL YEARS)*		-8,000.00	
TAXABLE PROFITS		62,000.00	11,780.00
CT SAVED	-1,520.00		-1,520.00
NET COST FOR THE COMPANY *(COST LESS CT SAVING)*	6,480.00		

NET COST AS A PERCENTAGE	81%

YOUR TAX POSITION			
	£	£	%
PROCEEDS FROM SELLING THE CAR		8,000.00	100%
TAX DUE ON THE PROCEEDS *(CARS ARE EXEMPT)*	NIL	-	0%
NET PROCEEDS RETAINED		8,000.00	100%

© PROFIT EXTRACTION, indicator

SECTION 6: PROS & CONS

ADVANTAGES OF SELLING TO THE COMPANY

1. Assets = no NI. When you sell a capital asset to the company there is no NI to pay on the profits you make on that transaction.

2. Tax-free. The first £8,500 of capital gains you make on selling an asset to the company is tax-free. There is no tax to pay when you sell an asset that is exempt from Capital Gains Tax to the company, such as a car.

3. Goods = NI savings. The NI you pay on profit you make on a trade in your own name by selling goods or services to the company is less than the NI you pay as an employed director of a company.

DISADVANTAGES OF SELLING TO THE COMPANY

1. Market value. When you sell a non tax-exempt asset to the company you are taxed as if you sold it for its market value however much you actually received.

2. Trading profit. When you sell goods or services to the company you are treated as carrying on a trade in your own name. You must pay income tax and self-employed NI on the profits of that trade.

3. Asset value. When you sell a valuable asset to the company any future increase in the value of that asset will be taxed within the company, possibly at a higher tax rate than would apply if the asset remained in your hands.

4. Disclosure. As a director of the company you are legally obliged to tell the other directors about any personal transactions you make with the company. Any significant transactions between you and the company must also be disclosed in a note to the company accounts.

Profit Extraction

Using a company pension fund

SECTION 1: METHOD

WHAT IS A COMPANY PENSION FUND?

By a company pension fund we mean a pool of investments just for the benefit of directors and/or key employees (up to a maximum of twelve). Such a fund is called a Small Self-Administered Scheme (SSAS) where the company maintains control over the investments made.

We are not considering Self-Invested Personal Pension Schemes (SIPPS), where the contributor can tell the pension provider how to invest the funds within certain legal limits. SIPPS have no profit extraction advantages over standard personal pension schemes (see Part 9).

HOW SHOULD YOU WITHDRAW COMPANY PENSION CONTRIBUTIONS?

The company can pay contributions into the pension scheme on your behalf in addition to any other salary and benefits it provides.

IS THERE A MAXIMUM THAT CAN BE PAID?

Taxman's formula. The amount the company can contribute to the SSAS on your behalf is based on the size of fund needed to pay you a pension on retirement. The current calculation for this is 1/30th of your final salary from the company, multiplied by the number of years you have worked for it, (up to a maximum of 2/3rds of that salary). Plus there needs to be enough in the fund to pay you a tax-free lump sum (on retirement) of 3/80ths of your final salary, again multiplied by the number of years you have worked.

Don't worry, a specialist adviser, the scheme's actuary, will work all this out for you.

Catching up. The company is permitted to pay extra contributions into the scheme to top up its funds if needed.

SECTION 2: YOUR COMPANY

IS A PENSION CONTRIBUTION TAX-DEDUCTIBLE FOR THE COMPANY?

Yes. Contributions made by the company are tax-deductible. The main condition is that the company must *pay* the contribution before its year-end.

WHAT IS THE NI COST?

None. There is no employers' NI on pension contributions paid into an approved company pension scheme.

Unapproved. If the pension scheme is not approved by the Taxman, the contributions made by the company are counted as part of your taxable income. In this case the company must report the contributions it makes on your P11D. However, the contribution is still tax-deductible for the company.

DOES IT MATTER HOW MUCH IS PAID IN ONE YEAR?

Annual contribution. The maximum contribution payable by the company is contained in the actuary's report on the scheme, which is generally updated every three years. Amounts paid in excess of this are treated as loans from the company to the fund and hence are not tax-deductible.

Special contributions. Sometimes the company can make a "special" contribution in order to top up the funds needed to, say, start paying out a pension. If you keep these "specials" to below £500,000 then the company will not have to spread the tax deduction over a number of years. You could easily exceed this limit if the company were to, say, transfer property into the SSAS instead of making a payment.

AMOUNT OF SPECIAL CONTRIBUTION	YEARS TAX DEDUCTION IS SPREAD OVER
£500,001 TO £1,000,000	2
£1,000,001 TO £2,000,000	3
OVER £2,000,000	4

USING A COMPANY PENSION FUND

SECTION 3: YOU

SHOULD CONTRIBUTIONS BE SHOWN ON YOUR TAX RETURN?

No. The contributions paid by the company on your behalf into an approved pension scheme are not treated as part of your income, so they should not be included on your tax return.

Unapproved. If the pension scheme is unapproved or loses approval, any contributions paid on your behalf by the company are treated as your income. In this case the contribution should be shown on your annual P11D. The amount of the contribution paid should also be shown on the "Employment" pages of your tax return in the section headed "Benefits and Expenses".

CAN YOU DEDUCT ANY EXPENSES FROM A PENSION CONTRIBUTION?

As the pension contribution paid by your company is not treated as your income, expenses paid by you cannot be deducted from the contribution.

WHAT IS THE NI COST?

None. Contributions paid by the company into an approved company pension scheme are not treated as part of your taxable income and there is no employees' NI charge due on those contributions.

Unapproved. Contributions paid into an unapproved scheme are subject to NI for you and the company.

AT WHAT RATE WILL YOU BE TAXED?

Approved. A pension contribution made by your company is not taxable on you. However, when you eventually receive a pension from the SSAS that will be taxed.

Unapproved. Contributions to an unapproved scheme are taxed as if they were part of your salary. The rate of income tax paid on an unapproved pension contribution will depend of the level of your taxable income for the tax year in which the contribution is paid.

© PROFIT EXTRACTION, Indicator

USING A COMPANY PENSION FUND

SECTION 4: VAT

ARE THERE ANY CONSEQUENCES FOR VAT?

No. There are no VAT implications whether or not the scheme has the Taxman's approval.

USING A COMPANY PENSION FUND

SECTION 5: EXAMPLE

This is an example of the tax-related consequences of withdrawing profits from your company in the form of contributions into a company pension fund.

We first look at what the payment of the pension contribution costs your company in net terms. We are taking into account the fact that the pension contribution is tax-deductible for the company.

We have used the following assumptions:

Pension contribution	£10,000
Corporation Tax (CT) rate paid by the company	19%
Your highest personal tax rate	40%

COMPANY'S TAX POSITION			
	£	**£**	**CT PAYABLE**
TAXABLE PROFIT BEFORE PAYMENT OF PENSION CONTRIBUTION		70,000.00	13,300.00
PENSION CONTRIBUTION PAID	10,000.00	-10,000.00	
NET PROFIT AFTER PENSION CONTRIBUTION		60,000.00	11,400.00
CT SAVED	-1,900.00		-1,900.00
NET COST FOR COMPANY (COST LESS CT SAVED)	8,100.00		

NET COST AS A PERCENTAGE	81%

YOUR TAX POSITION

A pension contribution made by your company is not taxable on you. However, your current net income doesn't increase either, unless it replaces a contribution you've already made. Of course when you eventually receive a pension from the SSAS that will be taxed.

© PROFIT EXTRACTION, Indicator

USING A COMPANY PENSION FUND

SECTION 6: PROS & CONS

ADVANTAGES OF A COMPANY PENSION SCHEME (SSAS)

1. Higher contributions. The company can pay more into a SSAS than the Taxman would allow to be paid into a personal pension scheme.

2. Control. The company can retain some control over the funds in the SSAS. For example, the SSAS can invest in property that the company then occupies and pays rent into the fund. The SSAS can also hold shares in the company if certain conditions are met.

3. Tax and NI-free. The contributions paid by the company into an approved company pension scheme are free of tax and NI.

4. Reduces Corporation Tax. The contributions paid by the company are tax-deductible so this reduces the amount of Corporation Tax it pays.

5. Lump sum. A company pension scheme can provide a bigger tax-free lump sum on retirement than is currently possible under a personal pension scheme.

DISADVANTAGE OF A COMPANY PENSION SCHEME (SSAS)

1. Locked-in. The pension contributions represent value that is locked into the pension scheme until you retire. A pension contribution paid on your behalf into a company pension scheme will provide you with no disposable income today. The level of pension the contribution will provide in the future is difficult to quantify, as it will depend on the performance of the investments in the SSAS.

Profit Extraction

Flexible dividends

SECTION 1: METHOD

WHAT DO WE MEAN BY A FLEXIBLE DIVIDEND?

Most companies are formed with shares of the same class (e.g. ordinary shares), which means if a dividend is paid, every shareholder gets a payment, not just you. By creating different classes of share you can pay each shareholder a different dividend or nothing at all. This is what is known as a flexible dividend.

If your shares are in a class (e.g. ordinary "A") of their own, you can pay more of the company's profit to yourself rather than having to pay other shareholders or resort to paying bonus.

HOW DO YOU SET UP A FLEXIBLE DIVIDEND?

Obviously, you have to create the different classes of share first. This is easily done without having to create new shares with different rights.

Existing shares. The shareholders hold an extraordinary general meeting and agree to reclassify the existing ordinary shares. You can call them "A" ordinary, "B" ordinary and "C" ordinary etc. until each shareholder has their own class. You can now vote a different dividend for each class of share. So if you hold the "A" shares you can take more of the profit by voting a higher dividend to the "A" shares only. You can even give a dividend to the "A" class alone.

Is it that easy? Yes, but with most things involving companies there are certain legal formalities, (see Appendix 3). If you feel you need more advice, a company secretarial specialist should be able to help you.

HOW MUCH DIVIDEND CAN YOU TAKE THIS WAY?

Out of profits. As with all dividends a company can only pay a flexible dividend if it has made a profit (that is not cancelled out by losses). The profit figure is the amount left after Corporation Tax has been deducted for the year, although you can pay a dividend out of profits left over from earlier years.

Approval. Each year the shareholders have to confirm that you should receive more of the profits because, say, you work full-time in the business. When a dividend is declared the Company Secretary must record the details in the company's minute book.

FLEXIBLE DIVIDENDS

© PROFIT EXTRACTION, Indicator

SECTION 2: YOUR COMPANY

IS A FLEXIBLE DIVIDEND TAX-DEDUCTIBLE FOR THE COMPANY?

No. Like other dividends this is paid out of the company's profits after the Corporation Tax due has been deducted. The payment of dividends has no affect on the amount of tax the company pays.

WHAT IS THE NI COST?

None. There is no employers' NI on flexible or other dividends.

SHOULD THE COMPANY DEDUCT TAX WHEN PAYING A FLEXIBLE DIVIDEND?

No. The company should not deduct tax when paying a flexible dividend.

Dividend vouchers. However, the company must prepare a dividend voucher to give to you when it's paid. The voucher shows the date the dividend is paid, the number of shares held, the amount paid and the income tax credit that attaches to it (see Appendix 1). These vouchers will help you when it comes to filling in your tax return.

Tax credit? With each dividend comes an income tax credit of one ninth of the amount paid. You are taxed on the gross amount of the dividend including the tax credit, but can offset it against all or some of the tax due.

ANY RESTRICTIONS ON PAYING A FLEXIBLE DIVIDEND?

Illegal dividend. As with any dividend if there are not enough retained profits in the company to make the payment, the Taxman will treat it as a loan to you (see Part 6).

IR35. If your company provides your personal services to other businesses it may be caught by the tax rules known as IR35. In this case if it pays out dividends in the same tax year it has to pay tax and NI on a "deemed salary" to you, it may be short of funds.

SECTION 3: YOU

SHOULD A FLEXIBLE DIVIDEND BE SHOWN ON YOUR TAX RETURN?

Yes. If you've been sent a personal tax return, the total amount of dividends received in a tax year should be shown under "Income from UK savings and investments". You need to collect together all the vouchers for dividends paid during the tax year and add up the figures of net dividend, tax credit and gross dividend. These three totals must be included in the main section of the tax return under the sub-heading "Dividends".

CAN YOU DEDUCT ANY EXPENSES FROM A FLEXIBLE DIVIDEND?

No. Expenses may only be deducted from earned income or rental income. A dividend is not earned income so you cannot deduct expenses from it.

WHAT IS THE NI COST?

None. There is no employees' NI on flexible or other dividends.

AT WHAT RATE WILL A FLEXIBLE DIVIDEND BE TAXED?

The amount of income tax due on any dividends you receive depends on the level of your total taxable income. Dividend income is always treated as if it sits on top of your pile of income. The income tax rates that apply to dividends received in 2005/06 are:

TAXATION OF DIVIDEND INCOME	
TAXABLE INCOME	TAX RATE
ON FIRST £32,400	10%
ABOVE £32,400	32.5%

Tax already paid? The tax credit on your dividend voucher does not represent all the income tax to be paid. The credit is just a device to ensure that shareholders who only pay tax at 10 or 22% do not pay any further tax on the dividends they receive, but if you pay tax at 40% there is more to pay.

FLEXIBLE DIVIDENDS

© PROFIT EXTRACTION, Indicator

SECTION 4: VAT

ARE THERE ANY CONSEQUENCES FOR VAT?

None. Withdrawing a flexible dividend from your company has no VAT consequences. Dividends paid to shareholders are not subject to VAT.

SECTION 5: EXAMPLE

This is an example of the tax-related consequences of withdrawing a flexible dividend from your company.

We first look at what the company must pay in Corporation Tax to have net profits available to pay the dividend. We will then calculate the net amount that you will be left with as an individual after deduction of income tax.

We have used the following assumptions:

Dividend withdrawn	£50,000
Corporation Tax (CT) rate paid by company	19%
Your highest personal tax rate on dividend	32.5%
Tax credit on dividend	1/9

You own 75% of the ordinary shares of your company, which means your share of the dividend is £37,500 (75% x £50,000). If you reclassify the ordinary shares as "A", "B", "C" etc. and your shares are the 'A' class then potentially the whole of the £50,000 dividend could be paid to you.

COMPANY'S TAX POSITION		
	£	**%**
AFTER-TAX PROFITS NEEDED TO PAY THE DIVIDEND	50,000.00	100.00%
CT PAYABLE TO ARRIVE AT THESE PROFITS ((£50,000 / 81) x 19)	11,728.40	
THEREFORE THE COMPANY HAS TO MAKE PROFITS BEFORE TAX OF ((£50,000 / 81) x 100)	61,728.40	123.45%

YOUR TAX POSITION						
	75% OF DIVIDEND (£)	**£**	**%**	**100% OF DIVIDEND (£)**	**£**	**%**
DIVIDEND WITHDRAWN	37,500.00	37,500.00	100%	50,000.00	50,000.00	100%
TAX CREDIT ON DIVIDEND (1/9)	4,166.67			5,555.55		
GROSS TAXABLE DIVIDEND	41,666.67			55,555.55		
INCOME TAX AT 32.5%	-13,541.67			-18,055.55		
OFFSET TAX CREDIT	4,166.67			5,555.55		
TOTAL TAXES		-9,375.00	25%		-12,500.00	25%
NET DIVIDEND AVAILABLE TO SPEND		28,125.00	75%		37,500.00	75%

Conclusion. From the above table you can see that your tax cost percentage is the same (i.e. 25%). However, you have increased your income by £9,372 (£37,500 - £28,125), whilst the company still pays the same total dividend of £50,000!

FLEXIBLE DIVIDENDS

© PROFIT EXTRACTION, Indicator

SECTION 6: PROS & CONS

ADVANTAGES OF FLEXIBLE DIVIDENDS

1. More of the profits. If your shares are in a class (e.g. ordinary "A") all of their own, you can pay more of the company's profit to yourself rather than other shareholders or resort to paying bonus.

2. No NI. There is no NI due on the payment of a dividend. There is no reason why you shouldn't pay yourself a little more than planned, being the 12.8% employers' NI you save the company by not taking a bonus. You can use this tactic year after year.

3. No further tax to pay. If your total income is less than £37,295 (£4,895 + £32,400) for the tax year 2005/06, you will have no further tax to pay on dividends you receive.

DISADVANTAGES OF FLEXIBLE DIVIDENDS

1. Pension contributions. Dividends are not earned income so they must be ignored when calculating the maximum that can be paid into a pension scheme.

2. May increase share value. Regular dividends paid at a high level can increase the value of your shareholding in the company. The value of large shareholdings will normally be based on the value of the assets less the liabilities the company holds. The value of smaller shareholdings will depend on the pattern of dividends the shareholders expect to receive. This could mean a larger Capital Gains Tax bill if you were to transfer shares to someone else.

3. Profits less than £50,000. From April 2004, the Corporation Tax paid by companies with profits below the small companies rate limit (£50,000 for a company without associates) depends on the level of dividends paid. This effects businesses with profits closer to zero than to £50,000.

FLEXIBLE DIVIDENDS

Profit Extraction

Royalties and licence fees

SECTION 1: METHOD

WHAT DO WE MEAN BY ROYALTIES AND LICENCE FEES?

Royalty. If you have a great idea for a new product or process you could apply for a patent for that invention in your own name. The company can then pay you for the right to exploit that patent by developing and marketing the product. Royalty fees are paid for the right to use a particular patent or trademark.

Licence. Alternatively you could think up a new design for one of your company's products and register it in your name, with the company paying you a licence fee for using it. Other examples are computer programs, manuals or books of any kind, all of which you write in your own time. Licence fees are payments for the use or exploitation of a copyright.

HOW DO YOU SET UP SUCH AN ARRANGEMENT?

Royalties and licence fees are similar in that they are both payments for the privilege of using some intellectual property that is protected by a patent or copyright. Setting them up, however, does have its differences.

Royalty. A patent is granted when an inventor registers a new product or process with the Patent Office. It is designed to give the inventor protection from someone else exploiting the idea without permission, for up to 20 years. To protect an invention internationally a patent must be acquired in each legal jurisdiction that it's likely to be used in.

Licence. Copyright applies automatically to works of an artistic nature such as literature, art and computer programs. It also covers unique designs, which may be registered under the **Copyright, Designs and Patents Act 1988** to give it protection similar to a patent. The copyright will endure for 25, 50 or even 70 years after the creator's death, depending on the nature of the work.

Legal agreement. It's important to have a legal agreement drawn up between you and the company to cover how much should be paid and for how long. The duration of the agreement will normally be for the period the company expects to market the product. It should contain a break-point at which both you or your company have an opportunity to renegotiate terms.

HOW MUCH CAN YOU WITHDRAW WITH THIS METHOD?

A commercial licence is normally granted in return for a percentage of sales, in the range of 5% to 20%. It's important that the Taxman can see that the licence fee has been calculated on a commercial basis and is not a disguised bonus or dividend from the company. So make the fee a percentage of turnover.

ROYALTIES AND LICENCE FEES

© PROFIT EXTRACTION, Indicator

SECTION 2: YOUR COMPANY

ARE THESE PAYMENTS TAX-DEDUCTIBLE FOR THE COMPANY?

Royalty. The payment of a royalty will reduce the amount of Corporation Tax (CT) paid by the company on its total profits for the year, but it cannot be used to turn a profit into a loss or increase tax losses. If the company has no taxable profits, the royalty payment is carried forward to be deducted in the next accounting period.

Licence fees paid for the use of copyright material or designs can be deducted from the company's profits to reduce the amount of CT it pays. There is no restriction about losses.

WHAT IS THE NI COST?

None. Royalties and licence fees paid to you are not subject to employers' NI.

SHOULD THE COMPANY DEDUCT INCOME TAX FROM THESE PAYMENTS?

Royalty. If the company pays you a royalty for the use of a patent held in your name it must deduct basic rate income tax at 22% before it pays the net amount to you. This tax is then paid over to the Taxman. The company should give you a certificate to show how much tax it has deducted from your royalty payments during a tax year.

Licence. If the company pays you a licence fee it is not required to deduct income tax.

Abroad. If you live outside the UK, the company should normally deduct basic rate tax from a licence fee. However, the company does not have to do so if that income is covered by a Double Taxation Agreement between the UK and the country you live in.

DOES IT MATTER HOW MUCH IS PAID?

Yes. The licence fee must be paid under a legal agreement between you and the company. The fee should be linked to the sales of the product that uses your copyright or patent, so the success of the product is your only restriction on how much is paid. If the fee is a percentage of profits it looks more like a dividend than a business expense and so the Taxman may not allow you to claim a royalty/licence fee as a tax deduction.

ROYALTIES AND LICENCE FEES

SECTION 3: YOU

SHOULD THIS INCOME BE SHOWN ON YOUR TAX RETURN?

Yes. Income earned from patents or copyrights should be shown on your tax return, under "Taxable income not entered elsewhere". You need to enter both the amount you received and any tax deducted by the company.

Trading. If you receive payments for the use of copyrights or patents from other sources, then this could be treated as a trade. Income and expenses would then be shown on the "Self-employment" pages of your tax return.

CAN YOU DEDUCT EXPENSES FROM THIS INCOME?

Royalty. When you register a patent you must pay an initial fee and each year thereafter keep it in force. The patent fees can be deducted from the income you receive.

Licence. A copyright is not granted but arises automatically, so there are no fees to pay unless you register a design. The cost of this can be deducted from your income.

Legal fees. The cost of drawing up a legal agreement between you and the company can also be deducted from the income you receive.

WHAT IS THE NI COST?

None. There is no employees' NI due on a royalty or licence fee paid to you by the company. As long as the terms of the formal agreement between you and your company are reasonable, the Taxman will not be able to argue that this is disguised remuneration, which would be subject to NI.

Self-employed. If you go down the trading route, NI will be due (see Part 16).

AT WHAT RATE WILL THIS INCOME FINALLY BE TAXED?

There are no special income tax rates for this type of income. This means that the rate of tax you finally pay depends on your total income during the tax year. The income tax rates on total taxable income for 2005/06 are: 10% on the first £2,090, 22% on the next £30,310 and 40% above £32,400.

HAS TAX ALREADY BEEN PAID ON THIS INCOME?

Royalty. The company must deduct basic rate tax at 22% from any royalty it pays and provide a certificate to show how much has been deducted in the tax year. You should enter on you own tax return the net amount of the royalty, the tax already deducted and the gross amount. This tax deducted at source will then reduce any additional tax you may have to pay on your income.

Licence. Unless you are normally resident overseas the company should not deduct tax from the licence fee it pays to you for the use of copyright material. This means no tax is paid up-front.

© PROFIT EXTRACTION, Indicator

ROYALTIES AND LICENCE FEES

SECTION 4: VAT

ARE THERE ANY CONSEQUENCES FOR VAT?

Your company. The VAT treatment of the grant of a licence will depend on where you, as the recipient of the fee, are based. If you live in a country outside the EU the company may have to account for VAT on the licence fee.

You. The grant of a licence to use copyright or patent material is not exempt from VAT. So if your total trading income exceeds the current VAT threshold of £60,000, (as from April 1, 2005) you must register as a VAT trader and charge VAT (see Part 16).

ROYALTIES AND LICENCE FEES

SECTION 5: EXAMPLE

This is an example of the tax-related consequences of withdrawing a licence fee from your company.

We first look at what the payment of the licence fee costs your company in net terms. We are taking into account the fact that the licence fee is tax-deductible for the company. We will then calculate the net amount that you will be left with as an individual after deduction of income tax.

We have used the following assumptions:

Licence fee paid	£5,000
Corporation Tax (CT) rate paid by the company	19%
Your highest personal tax rate	40%

COMPANY'S TAX POSITION			
	£	**£**	**CT PAYABLE**
TAXABLE PROFIT IN COMPANY BEFORE DEDUCTION OF LICENCE FEE		70,000.00	13,300.00
LICENCE FEE PAID	5,000.00	-5,000.00	
PROFIT AFTER LICENCE FEE		65,000.00	12,350.00
CT SAVED BY PAYING THE LICENCE FEE	-950.00		-950.00
NET COST TO THE COMPANY (COST LESS CT SAVED)	4,050.00		

NET COST AS A PERCENTAGE	81%

YOUR TAX POSITION			
	£	**£**	**%**
LICENCE FEE INCOME		5,000.00	100%
INCOME TAX AT 40% (ON £5,000)	2,000.00		
TOTAL TAX PAID		-2,000.00	40%
NET LICENCE FEE AVAILABLE TO SPEND		3,000.00	60%

© PROFIT EXTRACTION, Indicator

SECTION 6: PROS & CONS

ADVANTAGES OF ROYALTIES AND LICENCE FEES

1. NI saving. The company does not have to deduct employees' NI from the licence fee it pays to you, or pay any employers' NI either.

2. No tax deducted at source. If you live in the UK the company should not deduct tax from a licence fee it pays to you. However, it must deduct tax from any royalty payments.

3. Transferable. You can assign or transfer a copyright or patent you hold to another person, and so divert income that would normally be paid to you, to the person who holds the right.

4. Don't need profits. The licence fee should be related to the sales the company generates by using your copyright material or patented invention. So if the company makes a loss you should still receive the licence fee. Compare this to a dividend that can only be paid if the company makes a profit.

DISADVANTAGES OF ROYALTIES AND LICENCE FEES

1. In your name. You need to own the patent or copyright personally in order to receive the royalty or licence fee. So if the company initially spends money developing an idea you can't suddenly switch it into your name to generate income from it.

2. Cost. The cost of registering a patent can be quite steep. To fully protect the idea you will need to register patents in all countries where the invention or design is likely to be available. You also incur some costs in having a formal legal agreement drafted to cover the conditions under which the licence fee is paid and later renegotiated.

3. Publicity. Once the invention or design is registered certain details are made publicly available, including to your competitors. It can be very expensive to litigate against someone who produces a similar product.

ROYALTIES AND LICENCE FEES

Profit Extraction

Conclusion

SECTION 1: SUMMARY OF NUMBERS

In this section we've put togther a summary of the main examples given in each part of the book. Each one represents a particular profit extraction method.

HOW CAN THE VARIOUS METHODS BE COMPARED?

We have set our comparison out in the form of a table showing what each method costs your company and the after-tax income that you're left with. Here's a guide to the various columns in the table:

Column 1. In this column is the method and the part of the book it appears in.

Column 2. In this column, for each method, is the percentage cost to your company of providing you with the amount you wish to withdraw. If the company starts at 100% this is the net cost to it after allowing for a Corporation Tax (CT) deduction. For example:

- **123.45%.** This means there is no CT saving with this method. In fact you have to pay more in taxes to arrive at the figure (i.e.100%), than you are extracting. This applies to dividends in particular, which are paid out of post-CT profits. To pay a £10,000 dividend the company has to have made a £12,345 profit, which after CT (at 19%) of £2,345 gives you the dividend that can be paid.

- **81%.** This means that the cost of providing you with income under this particular method is offset by a saving for the company of 19% in CT. For £10,000 paid this way it really only costs the company £8,100.

- **91.37%.** This means that employers' NI was added to the cost before the CT saving of 19% was taken off. There is employers' NI on most benefits-in-kind such as company cars, medical expenses and free accommodation. Also for these benefits, there are unusual tax calculations which distort the percentages e.g. company cars.

- **0.5%.** Means that there is little cost to the company in providing you with income under this method.

Column 3. In this column, we show for each method, the percentage of income you get to keep after taxes. Again it is out of 100%. For example:

- **100%.** Means that this source of income is both tax and NI-free for you.

- **75%.** As a higher rate taxpayer this is what you eventually get to keep out of a dividend that is paid to you. Initially you get more, however, any income tax due is paid later via your tax return.

- **60%.** Means only income tax at 40% is taken from you.

Column 4. This shows the gross income that is required to give you an increase in net income of £10,000.

Column 5. This shows the cost to your company of providing the income shown in column 4.

The main assumptions we have made are that the company pays CT at the rate of 19% and that you're a 40% taxpayer.

© PROFIT EXTRACTION, Indicator

COLUMN 1	COLUMN 2	COLUMN 3	COLUMN 4	COLUMN 5
PROFIT EXTRACTION METHOD	**NET COST TO YOUR COMPANY (%)**	**HOW MUCH YOU GET TO KEEP (%)**	**GROSS AMOUNT OF INCOME REQUIRED TO GIVE £10,000 NET INCREASE (£)**	**WHAT COLUMN 4 COSTS YOUR COMPANY (£)**
PART 1: SALARY	86.95	69.61	14,366	12,490
PART 2: BONUS	86.01	59	16,949	14,578
PART 3: DIVIDENDS	123.45	75	13,333	16,460
PART 4: INTEREST	81	60	16,667	13,500
PART 5: RENT	81	60	16,667	13,500
PART 6: LOANS	0.5	98	10,204	10,000
PART 7: COMPANY CARS	97.66	48	20,833	20,346
PART 8: MILEAGE CLAIMS	81	100	10,000	8,100
PART 9: PERSONAL PENSIONS	81	100	10,000	8,100
PART 10: USING COMPANY ASSETS	83.07	92	10,870	9,030
PART 11: FREE ACCOMMODATION	91.37	60	16,667	15,229
PART 12: CHILDCARE	86.37	77.04	12,980	11,211
PART 13: MEDICAL EXPENSES	91.37	60	16,667	15,229
PART 14: FAMILY DIVIDEND	123.45	80	12,500	15,431
PART 15: FAMILY SALARY	91.37	63	15,873	14,503
PART 16: SELLING TO YOUR COMPANY	81	54.35	18,399	14,903
PART 17: USING A COMPANY PENSION FUND	81	100	10,000	8,100
PART 18: FLEXIBLE DIVIDENDS	123.45	75	13,333	16,460
PART 19: ROYALTIES AND LICENCE FEES	81	60	16,667	13,500

The above table allows you to look up a particular method and see what you get to keep. You can also see how much that would cost your company. However, to look at the total tax cost (to both you and your company) we have extended the table onto the next page.

Column 1. In this column is the method and the part of the book it appears in.

Column 6. To receive £10,000 extra income after personal taxes this is the total amount of tax you would pay.

Column 7. To provide you with that extra £10,000 net there is a tax cost to the company. However, this is wholly or partly offset by any tax deduction it gets for using this method.

Column 8. The combined total of your personal tax cost and the company's additional cost/(tax saving).

COLUMN 1	COLUMN 6	COLUMN 7	COLUMN 8
PROFIT EXTRACTION METHOD	FOR £10,000 NET, YOUR TAX COST (£)	YOUR COMPANY'S (TAX SAVING)/ADDITIONAL COST (£)	TOTAL TAX COST/(SAVING) (£)
PART 1: SALARY	4,365	(1,875)	2,490
PART 2: BONUS	6,949	(2,371)	4,578
PART 3: DIVIDENDS	3,333	3,127	6,460
PART 4: INTEREST	6,667	(3,167)	3,500
PART 5: RENT	6,667	(3,167)	3,500
PART 6: LOANS	204	(204)	0
PART 7: COMPANY CARS	10,833	(487)	10,346
PART 8: MILEAGE CLAIMS	0	(1,900)	(1,900)
PART 9: PERSONAL PENSIONS	0	(1,900)	(1,900)
PART 10: USING COMPANY ASSETS	870	(1,840)	(970)
PART 11: FREE ACCOMMODATION	6,667	(1,438)	5,229
PART 12: CHILDCARE	2,980	(1,769)	1,211
PART 13: MEDICAL EXPENSES	6,667	(1,438)	5,229
PART 14: FAMILY DIVIDEND	2,500	2,931	5,431
PART 15: FAMILY SALARY	5,873	(1,370)	4,503
PART 16: SELLING TO YOUR COMPANY	8,399	(3,496)	4,903
PART 17: USING A COMPANY PENSION FUND	0	(1,900)	(1,900)
PART 18: FLEXIBLE DIVIDENDS	3,333	3,127	6,460
PART 19: ROYALTIES AND LICENCE FEES	6,667	(3,167)	3,500

The main assumptions we have made are that the company pays CT at the rate of 19% and that you're a 40% taxpayer.

© PROFIT EXTRACTION, Indicator

SECTION 2: SUMMARY OF THE TEXT

In this section we've put togther a summary of the text given in each part of the book. In the table on the following pages each row represents a particular profit extraction method.

Each column in the table represents a key question when making comparisons between methods. We've tried to keep to simple Yes or No answers. Of course, if you want more detail, you can go back to the individual Parts. We recommend making use of the Contents page (which also lists all the questions asked) to do this.

	DEDUCTIBLE FOR THE COMPANY?	INCOME TAX PAYABLE?	EMPLOYERS' NI?	EMPLOYEES' NI?
SALARY	YES	YES	YES	YES
BONUS	YES	YES	YES	YES
DIVIDENDS	NO	YES	NO	NO
INTEREST	YES	YES	NO	NO
RENT	YES	YES	NO	NO
LOANS	NO	ON NOTIONAL INTEREST ONLY	ON NOTIONAL INTEREST ONLY	NO
COMPANY CARS	YES	YES	YES	NO
MILEAGE CLAIMS	YES	IN PRINCIPLE NO	NO	IN PRINCIPLE NO
PERSONAL PENSIONS	YES	NO	NO	NO
USING COMPANY ASSETS	YES	YES (ON 20% OF VALUE)	YES	NO
FREE ACCOMMODATION	YES	YES (ANNUAL VALUE)	YES	NO
CHILDCARE	YES	YES	NO	NO
MEDICAL EXPENSES	YES	YES	NO	NO
FAMILY DIVIDEND	NO	NO	NO	NO
FAMILY SALARY	YES	NO	YES	YES
SELLING TO YOUR COMPANY	YES	YES	NO	SELF-EMPLOYED NI
USING A COMPANY PENSION FUND	YES	NO	NO	NO
FLEXIBLE DIVIDENDS	NO	YES	NO	NO
ROYALTIES AND LICENCE FEES	YES	YES	NO	NO

© PROFIT EXTRACTION, Indicator

CONCLUSION

Consequences for VAT?	Tax return entry?	Can you do this each year?	Difficult to arrange in practice?	Comments
NONE	YES	YES	NO	
NONE	YES	YES	NO	
NONE	YES	YES	NO	TAX COST FOR PROFITS UNDER £50,000
NONE	YES	YES	NO	CHARGE A COMMERCIAL RATE
IT VARIES	YES	YES	YOU NEED A PROPERTY	
NONE	YES	YES	NO	THE LOAN IS REPAYABLE
IT VARIES	YES	YES	NO	IT DEPENDS ON THE CAR
IT VARIES	YES	YES	NO	BUSINESS MILEAGE ONLY
NONE	NO	YES	NO	LONG-TERM OPTION
IT VARIES	YES	YES	NO	YOU DON'T OWN THEM
IT VARIES	YES	YES	NO	
NONE	YES	YES	NO	FIRST £50 P.W. IS TAX AND NI-FREE
NONE	YES	YES	NO	AVOID REIMBURSEMENT
NONE	NO	YES	NO	FAMILY MEMBER TAXED
NONE	NO	YES	NO	FAMILY MEMBER TAXED
IT VARIES	YES	YES	NO	
NONE	NO	YES	NO	LONG-TERM OPTION
NONE	YES	YES	NO	RECLASSIFY SHARES FIRST
NONE	YES	YES	NO	

© PROFIT EXTRACTION, Indicator

SECTION 3: SELECTION PROCESS

This book can be used as a source of reference to dip into as and when required. However, it's best used to help you plan the most tax-effective way of extracting profit from your company in the future. We've compared each of the methods on the basis of how much they cost your company and the amount of net income you end up with. Armed with this information you will now be able to produce a tax-effective profit extraction strategy. We suggest you do this in two stages, as follows:

Step 1. Eliminate. Eliminate those methods you're not interested in. This could be because you just don't think the method will suit your particular situation. This will leave you with a shortlist of relevant methods.

Step 2. Maximising your income. We suggest you try and improve your current situation, choosing from the most tax-efficient first. But how can you tell? In the following table we have ranked our profit extraction methods in order of tax cost. The figures shown are the combined tax cost for you and your company by taking £10,000 of profit out, using a particular method.

There are some examples (in section 4) below of how our selection process works in practice.

RANKING	METHOD	PART	TOTAL TAX COST/(SAVING) (£)
1	MILEAGE CLAIMS	8	(1,900)
2	PERSONAL PENSIONS	9	(1,900)
3	USING A COMPANY PENSION FUND	17	(1,900)
4	USING COMPANY ASSETS	10	(970)
5	LOANS	6	0
6	CHILDCARE	12	1,211
7	SALARY	1	2,490
8	INTEREST	4	3,500
9	RENT	5	3,500
10	ROYALTIES AND LICENCE FEES	19	3,500
11	FAMILY SALARY	15	4,503
12	BONUS	2	4,576
13	SELLING TO YOUR COMPANY	16	4,903
14	FREE ACCOMMODATION	11	5,229
15	MEDICAL EXPENSES	13	5,229
16	FAMILY DIVIDEND	14	5,431
17	DIVIDENDS	3	6,460
18	FLEXIBLE DIVIDENDS	18	6,460
19	COMPANY CARS	7	10,346

WHY DO DIVIDENDS HAVE SUCH A LOW RANKING?

Dividends have such a low ranking because they are paid out of after-tax profits. This means you have to make even more profits (e.g. 123% for a company paying 19% Corporation Tax) to pay the amount you want. Therefore, dividends save on NI but cost the company more in profits.

CONCLUSION

© PROFIT EXTRACTION, Indicator

SECTION 4: EXAMPLES

Example 1 - making more of what you've got

Your current situation. You currently extract £50,000 of your company's profit as salary, which gives you net income of £34,803. Can you improve on this by using a combination of salary and other profit extraction methods? The answer is yes, but by which combination?

Step 1. Eliminate.

- Company car

- Childcare

- Interest

- Medical expenses

- Flexible dividend

- Pension contribution

- Mileage claim

Step 2. Maximising. From the seven methods you liked the look of you have chosen the three most tax-efficient ones.

1. Interest. You have lent money to the company and decided to charge it interest at 10% p.a.

2. Flexible dividend. As you have other shareholders you decided to reclassify the ordinary shares to allow the majority of dividends to be paid just to you alone.

3. Pension contribution. You've decided to top up your pension contribution by £1,500, paid for by the company.

4. Basic salary. You've decided to keep a basic salary that uses up your personal tax-free allowance and 10% income tax band for this year. It stops short of pushing you into the 40% tax bracket, until you add the other extraction methods.

Method	Gross income (£)	Percentage	Net income (£)
Interest	2,000	98%	1,960
Flexible dividend	9,250	75%	6,937
Pension contribution	1,500	100%	1,500
Basic salary*	37,250	About 69%	25,702
Total gross income	**50,000**	**Total net income**	**36,099**

***Basic salary.** We have taken a basic salary to be one that keeps you just below the 40% tax bracket. For 2005/06 this is £32,400 plus your tax-free allowance of £4,895 which together give a salary of £37,295. We've taken £37,250 for illustrative purposes.*

CONCLUSION

Conclusion. By moving away from salary to other methods you have increased your net income by £1,500 (£36,169 - £34,669).

EXAMPLE 2 - TAKING JUST A LITTLE BIT MORE

Your current situation.

You need to increase your net income by £2,500 a month (£30,000 a year). You can achieve this by using a combination of profit extraction methods. But which ones?

Step 1. Eliminate.

- Flexible dividend

- Interest

- Childcare

- Medical expenses

Step 2. Maximisation. From the four methods you liked the look of you have chosen the two most tax-efficient ones.

1. Flexible dividend. As you have other shareholders you decided to reclassify the ordinary shares to allow the majority of dividends to be paid just to you alone.

2. Interest. You have lent money to the company and have decided to charge it interest at 10% p.a.

METHOD	EXTRA AFTER-TAX INCOME YOU WANT (£)	PERCENTAGE PER TABLE	GROSSING UP*	GROSS INCOME FROM YOUR COMPANY (£)
INTEREST	10,000	60	(10,000/60) x 100	16,667
FLEXIBLE DIVIDEND	20,000	75	(20,000/75) x 100	26,667
TOTAL NET INCOME	**30,000**			**43,334**

Grossing up is (income/% age) x 100

Conclusion. To gain an extra £30,000 of net income using these two methods your company needs to pay you an extra £43,334.

Compare this to an after-tax bonus of £30,000 which requires a gross payment of £50,847 (£30,000/59 x 100). On top of which there would be employers' NI of £6,508. Total cost £57,355. If the company pays Corporation Tax (CT) at 19% the net cost to it is £46,457 (100% - 19% = 81% x £57,355).

The net cost (after saving CT) to the company of paying interest of £10,000 is £8,100 (100% - 19% = 81% x £10,000). So a tax saving of £1,900.

To pay a dividend of £20,000 the company needs to have made pre-CT profits of £24,690. So a tax cost of £4,690.

© PROFIT EXTRACTION, Indicator

CONCLUSION

TAX COST TO YOUR COMPANY		
METHOD	**YOUR CHOICE**	**BONUS ALTERNATIVE**
INTEREST	(1,900)	
FLEXIBLE DIVIDEND	4,690	
BONUS EMPLOYERS' NI		5,271*
TOTAL COST TO THE COMPANY	**2,790**	**5,271**

(100% - 19% = 81% x £6,508).

Profit Extraction

Timing

SECTION 1: METHOD

WHAT DO WE MEAN BY TIMING?

There will be a flow of money between you and your company – relating to salary, travel, rent, dividends etc. Amongst these could be a number of profit extraction methods which best suit your circumstances. Having decided on which methods to use there remains the question of which order to arrange them in.

You. The Taxman's PAYE system is waiting in the wings to take income tax and NI from you on a monthly (or possibly weekly) basis. For you, timing means getting your hands on the results of a particular profit extraction method as quickly as possible. Whilst on the other hand, trying to delay for as long as possible the date you'll have to pay over the related tax. This gives you the opportunity to put the money you will ultimately pay across to good use (for example, using it to reduce private borrowings and hence save on interest charges). Better in your pocket than the Taxman's! This could mean delaying the start of a particular profit extraction method until the beginning (April 6) of the next tax year and using others first during the current tax year.

We suggest that each month you take the items that are both tax and NI-free first. Only take a monthly dividend if you know there's enough after tax profit in the company to pay it. Other things you can catch up on at the end of the tax year.

Your company. Your company pays Corporation Tax (CT), on its profits nine months after its year-end. By putting alternative profit extraction methods in place before the year-end you'll be in a position to reduce that CT bill. Otherwise you'll have to wait, say, another 21 months for the profit extraction method to have an impact. Why 21 months? That's another twelve-month accounting period of your company plus nine months, before a CT bill is due again. Broadly the action your company needs to do falls into the following points in time, which are before:

1. its year-end
2. the accounts for that year are finalised
3. nine months have elapsed after the year-end
4. the end of the tax year i.e. April 5.

Documentation. The rules of most companies, the Articles of Association, require the shareholders to agree on major aspects of company policy such as directors' remuneration. Usually this is evidenced by voting on a resolution or two at the company's Annual General Meeting. However, in practice, the company will pay amounts to you before this meeting happens. You should therefore record, in a director's board minute, the level of e.g. bonus, that has been agreed for the year, before you take it. Unfortunately bookkeeping entries in the accounts that show the outcome of your decisions will not be enough if challenged by the Taxman.

Director's loan account. You could leave what you are entitled to within the company, so that the company credits the relevant amount to your director's current account. It is then available for you to draw at any time you want. However, you will be taxed as if the company had given you a cheque on the date it's put into your director's current account.

SECTION 2: YOUR COMPANY

WILL THE PROFIT EXTRACTION METHOD BE TAX DEDUCTIBLE FOR YOUR COMPANY?

Most of the methods recommended in this book are tax deductible for the company. A quick reminder is given in column 1 of the table on page 172.

WHEN WILL YOUR COMPANY GET A TAX DEDUCTION?

Making a provision. Your company pays Corporation Tax (CT) on its profits (for an accounting period) nine months after its year-end. The starting point to calculate how much CT it will pay, is the profit before tax figure shown in its final accounts. If you can get the cost of your profit extraction method included in those accounts as an expense, it will reduce the CT bill sooner rather than later.

If the company has an obligation to pay the sum at its year-end then it can provide for that expense when finalising its accounts for that year – even if it hasn't paid the money across yet.

The main exceptions to this rule to watch out for are:

1. **Salary and bonus.** If you make a provision for salary or bonus in the year-end accounts of your company, the PAYE due on these must be paid within nine months of that year-end. If it isn't then these get added back to the company's profits by the Taxman, which will in turn increase the company's CT bill.

2. **Pension contributions.** It's the amount of pension premium paid by the company before its year-end that counts, not what it is obliged to pay. For example:

   > If the company draws up its accounts to December 31, 2005, any pension contribution for 2005 must be paid by December 31 to be set against the profits made in the 2005 set of accounts. A contribution is therefore an ideal way to reduce the taxable profit of the company before the financial year-end has passed.

3. **Royalties.** The payment of a royalty to you will reduce the amount of CT paid by the company on its total profits for its accounting period, but it cannot be used to turn a profit into a loss or increase tax losses. If the company has no taxable profits, the royalty payment is carried forward to be deducted in the next accounting period.

DOES IT MATTER IF THE COMPANY PAYS YOU MONTHLY, QUARTERLY OR ANNUALLY?

No. The company will still get its tax deduction. However, in March each year it's worthwhile checking whether any payments have to be made before the end of the tax year (April 5).

The amount of NI-free salary (£94 for 2005/06) is normally set out as a weekly figure, which changes in April each year.

WHEN WILL ANY EMPLOYERS' NI BE PAYABLE?

A quick reminder of which methods attract employers' NI is given in column 3 of the table on page 172.

If you plan to extract profits by way of benefits-in-kind your company will have to pay the Taxman, by July 6 each year, employers' NI (currently at the rate of 12.8%) on their value. This relates to the tax year not the company year i.e. it's benefits made available to you between April 6 in one year and April 5 in the next.

WHEN CAN THE COMPANY PAY A DIVIDEND?

Your need for cash may dictate the regular payment of dividends by your company to you. These are known as interim dividends whose typical timing is quarterly, though there is an increasing fashion for monthly dividends to be paid. A final divided can also be paid to you once the reserves for the year are known (from the final accounts), but payment of this is linked to the company's Annual General Meeting (AGM). The point is that for either an interim or final dividend to be validly paid requires distributable reserves. If the company has these then it can pay that dividend. At the time a dividend is declared the company's financial records must be adequate to demonstrate this is the case. Reliable management accounts will normally satisfy this requirement.

Having established the availability of reserves your company needs to follow the appropriate procedure depending on whether the dividend is interim or final. Note that the Taxman may challenge dividends not properly declared and paid in accordance with company law.

Interim dividends. For interim dividends a company regulation (check your company's Articles of Association to make sure this clause is there), normally gives directors the power to pay a dividend if it is justified by profit. So for an interim dividend hold a board meeting and prepare minutes approving the payment. When the company makes the payment it's good practice to issue a dividend voucher (see Appendix 1) at the same time.

Director's loan account. Interim dividends are treated by the Taxman as "made" when cheques are issued to you (as a shareholder) or when funds are at your disposal by way of an accounting entry in the company's books e.g. posted as a credit to your director's loan account.

Final dividend. Only the shareholders of the company can approve a final dividend. For such a dividend: (1) the company secretary will (before the general meeting) need to prepare documents recommending a dividend; (2) at the general meeting itself the shareholders must formally approve the dividends recommended (including the interim dividends already declared); and (3) minutes need to be prepared as evidence that all of this actually happened.

A final dividend is treated as declared on the date of the AGM, if no specific (later) date for payment is fixed at that AGM. Again when the company makes the dividend payment it's good practice to send a dividend voucher (see Appendix 1) at the same time.

© PROFIT EXTRACTION, Indicator

TIMING

SECTION 3: YOU

WILL THE PROFIT EXTRACTION METHOD RESULT IN A TAX BILL FOR YOU?

Most of the methods recommended in this book are taxable on you. A quick reminder is given in column 2 of the table on page 172. Column 3 will tell you if there is any employees' NI due.

WHEN DO YOU HAVE TO NOTIFY THE TAXMAN?

The entries you make on your annual tax return are sufficient notice to the Taxman of your sources of income in any one tax year (April 5 to April 6). This includes the results of the profit extraction methods you have chosen.

If salary, bonus and/or benefits-in-kind are taken during the tax year, the Taxman will already have been notified of the relevant amounts through your company's annual PAYE returns i.e. the P35 with accompanying P14s (your copy of this is a P60) and P11Ds for expenses and benefits.

Salary and/or bonus. A bonus is taxable in the year in which it is awarded or paid out. This is not necessarily the same year as the company gets a tax deduction for it.

Example.

In the calendar year 2004 your company made a £50,000 profit. During the finalising of the accounts you decide to award a £20,000 bonus in June 2005. That bonus will be deductible for your company in 2004, even though it is not awarded until 2005. For its 2004 accounting year, your company will be taxed on £30,000 (£50,000 - £20,000).

However, you will not be taxed on your bonus until June 2005 (year of assessment 2005/06) because it was not awarded or paid out until then. This means it will go on your 2005/06 tax return.

Dividends. If you complete a tax return the total amount of dividends you received during a tax year should be shown under "Income from UK savings and investments". You need to collect all the vouchers for dividends paid during the tax year and add up the figures of net dividend, tax credit and gross dividend. These three totals must be included under the sub-heading "Dividends".

Interest. The interest you receive from the company between April 6, 2005 and April 5, 2006 ends up on your 2005/06 tax return, under "Income from UK savings and investments". You should copy the amount of net interest paid from the certificate (see Appendix 2) provided by the company, to your tax return. The key thing here is that the interest has to be paid to you by the company for you to be taxed on it. For example, delaying an interest payment until after April 6, 2006 means you won't be taxed on it until January 2008.

TIMING

Rent. Any rent due to you from the company between April 6, 2005 and April 5, 2006 is income from land or property. If the property is in the UK you should include the rent on "Land and Property" supplementary pages with your 2005/06 tax return. If the property is abroad (e.g. a villa in Spain) you should fill in details of the rents received and expenses set against those rents on the "Foreign Income" supplementary pages for that return.

Gains. If you sell a capital asset to the company between April 6, 2005 and April 5, 2006 you must report this on the "Capital Gains" pages of a tax return. However, if all the gains you make total less than £8,500 (for 2005/06), you do not have to report them. You are also saved the bother of making an entry on these pages if the assets are: (1) cars; (2) property you occupied within the last three years as your main home; (3) government stocks known as gilts; (4) foreign currency; and (5) moveable possessions (known as chattels) sold for less than £6,000.

WHEN WILL ANY INCOME TAX AND NI DUE HAVE TO BE PAID?

If you change your profit extraction methods in 2005/06 then any additional tax payable on your total income is due by January 31, 2007. However, the Taxman assumes thereafter that your income will remain constant and so asks for payments on account of the next year's tax bill on January 31 and July 31.

Again, for changes to profit extraction levels in 2006/07 any additional tax due is payable by January 31, 2008.

Paid under PAYE. Any income tax and NI due on a regular salary or one off bonus should already have been collected through the PAYE system.

© PROFIT EXTRACTION, Indicator

TIMING

SECTION 4: VAT

ARE THERE ANY CONSEQUENCES FOR VAT?

You. There are no VAT consequences for you when considering timing.

Your company. Some of the benefits-in-kind reported on the P11D are VAT-inclusive. This is even if the company has been able to recover the VAT. So a record of the VAT-inclusive price needs to be maintained.

SECTION 5: EXAMPLE

Assumptions. Let's say for 2005/06 you've got £5,000 worth of profit to take out each month. The methods you've decided on are: a low monthly salary for you (and family employees), tax-free mileage expenses, rent and dividends. However, what should you pay yourself first?

MONTHLY

Basic (family) salaries. Salary/wages of up to £94 per week is tax and NI-free. Pay this £407 first each month. If you and your spouse are both employees of the company then that's £814 out of the extraction budget.

Mileage expenses. You are running your own car but charge the company for business miles. How many miles can you pay at 40p a mile this month?

Other expenses. If the money is in the bank by all means reimburse yourself for costs incurred on behalf of the company. At the same time, if it has paid some of your bills (e.g. home phone) pay the company back for any private element of those bills. Always make sure the bill is in the company's name to avoid a PAYE problem.

Rent. Take out the monthly rent (and don't forget the quarterly service charge if applicable). If your company hasn't got the cash for this, it can build up an arrears until it can afford to pay. The tax situation is still the same i.e. the company gets a tax deduction for and you are taxed on the rent due, not just what has been paid. Start a rent increase at the beginning of a tax year – lease permitting of course. This way you don't pay tax on the increase until nine months after the end of the tax year.

Regular dividends. Is this a month in which you should take a dividend? Company law says you can pay these if you know you've made enough profit to cover them (after Corporation Tax (CT)). For example, if you prepare accurate quarterly management accounts use them but be conservative. One method is to take only 80% of the accounts profit, knock off 19% for CT and use the balance to pay a dividend. This way you have a cushion in case there is a downturn in future profitability. For example, a profit of £5,000 means you would only take a dividend of £3,240 (£5,000 x 80% = £4,000 less CT at 19%) to err on the side of caution. If you haven't used last year's profit up you can pay a dividend out of that instead.

As this is an interim dividend hold a board meeting and prepare minutes approving the payment. When the company makes the payment it issues you with a dividend voucher (see Appendix 1) at the same time. If the payment has to be delayed because of cash flow reasons, have the dividend posted as a credit to your director's loan account and draw down on this as and when the company is back in funds.

TIMING

© PROFIT EXTRACTION, Indicator

BEFORE YOUR COMPANY'S YEAR-END

During the last two months of your company's financial year consider…

Pension contributions. Although you didn't select it as one of your preferred methods of profit extraction, consider whether the company can afford to pay a contribution into your pension plan. If it pays this before the end of its financial year this will reduce any CT it has to pay in nine months time.

Assets for your use. If the company wants to lend you any assets to use (e.g. a laptop computer) it will get an earlier tax deduction for their acquisition cost if it acquires them before its year-end, rather than shortly afterwards.

BEFORE THE ACCOUNTS ARE FINALISED

As part of the final adjustments to your company's annual accounts before they are approved and signed off by the directors, consider…

Bonuses. Making a provision for directors' and other employees' bonuses to reduce the profit and hence the CT payable on those accounts.

Expenses. Including accruals in the accounts for any expenses due to you that were unpaid at the year-end.

BEFORE THE NINE-MONTH DEADLINE

Salaries and bonuses. In order for your company to get a deduction for the salary and bonus related figures included in its accounts, make sure that any tax or NI due on those has been paid within nine months of that year-end.

Final dividend. You've taken interim dividends so far. After the accounts have been finalised is the time to consider taking a final dividend out of the company. Remember only the shareholders of the company can approve a final dividend so the date of this will be linked to when you hold the company's Annual General Meeting.

BEFORE THE END OF THE TAX YEAR

In March of each year it will be time for...

Payments. For example, paying the 5p passenger mileage rate, repaying any private fuel, a mileage claim for business miles you overlooked, and making good any benefits-in-kind (other than company cars) you don't want to be taxed on.

SECTION 6: PROS & CONS

ADVANTAGES OF TIMING

One off. When you start using a new profit extraction method there can be a 21-month delay in having to pay the personal tax bill on it. For example, if you start charging your company a monthly rent on April 6, 2006 then you won't have a tax bill to pay on that until January 31, 2008. Thereafter you'll be asked to make payments on account of your total tax bill (provided it exceeds £500) each July and January as long as you have this source of income.

DISADVANTAGES OF TIMING

Tax cash. Delaying tax bills means you'll need to remember to organise payment of them at some future date. If the money isn't there when it's eventually due you might need to resort to another round of profit extraction; sufficient to put you in funds to settle your account with the Taxman.

Regular dividends. If you are going to pay regular interim dividends you'll need accurate quarterly management accounts to avoid the risk of them being classed as illegal dividends (where the dividends exceed the final profits available for distribution). However, there will of course be an administration cost to produce these management accounts.

© PROFIT EXTRACTION, Indicator

Profit Extraction

Appendices

ABC LIMITED

Directors: Mr A   1 Any Road
                   Mrs B   Any Town
                   Ms C   ABC1 1ABC

                                                                                  [Date]

[Name of shareholder]
[Address]

Dear **[Name]**

Dividend for the period ending [DD/MM/YY] *[your financial year-end]*

We give below the details of the dividend payment made to you on *[date]*.

Number of shares: *[X]* ordinary shares of £1 *[nominal value]*

Dividend rate: *[X%]*

Total dividend for the period ending *[DD/MM/YY]*:   *[£X]*

Total tax credit: *[£X]*

Remember to keep this voucher with your tax records. It supports the dividend entries you make on your self-assessment tax return.

Yours sincerely
On behalf of ABC Limited

Ms D
Secretary

Note: Tax Credit is dividend paid x 1/9 e.g. on a paid dividend of £900 the tax credit would be £100. Gross dividend £1,000 (net £900 plus tax credit £100). You don't have to do anything with this other than record it on the voucher.

APPENDIX 2: ANNUAL CERTIFICATE OF INTEREST

ABC Limited
Any Town
ABC1 1ABC

[Date]

[Name]
[Address]

Dear **[Name]**

Interest Certificate for the period April 6 [Year] to April 5 [Year]

Below is the interest you earned for the last tax year, which was paid to you or credited to your loan account.

Interest before tax: (Gross interest)	£*[XX.XX]*
Tax paid:	£*[XX.XX]*
Interest after tax: (Net interest)	£*[XX.XX]*

Please note that any tax deducted was based on the basic rate of tax and then paid direct to the Inland Revenue. The amount of interest actually paid to you or added to your account was the interest after tax.

Tax return. Remember to keep this certificate with your tax records. It supports interest-received entries you make on your self-assessment tax return.

Yours sincerely
On behalf of ABC Limited

Ms D
Secretary

APPENDICES

APPENDIX 3: FLEXIBLE DIVIDENDS
COMPANIES HOUSE FORMALITIES

You will need to pass an ordinary resolution reclassifying shares to allow for flexible dividends. The steps involved in this are as follows:

STEP 1. HOLDING AN EGM

EGM. An extraordinary general meeting (EGM) of a company's shareholders has to be convened when there is special business to be dealt with by the members – if this can't be covered at the annual general meeting (AGM).

Notice. Once the board has decided to hold a general meeting the company secretary must prepare the notice of the meeting and send a copy of it to each director, shareholder and the auditor (if you have one). The notice must say what business will be conducted at the meeting, as well as where and when it is to be held. Twenty-one clear days' notice must be given of the meeting, excluding the day of posting and the day of the meeting. But check the company's Articles of Association to see what they say about notice for meetings for your particular company.

Tip. Short notice. It is possible to convene a general meeting without giving the full 21 days notice if all the shareholders who are entitled to vote agree. Such agreement should preferably be in writing, to avoid any later dispute.

STEP 2. PASSING A RESOLUTION

Ordinary resolution. The meeting has to pass an "ordinary" resolution to reclassify the share capital into different classes of shares as held by the different shareholders. Passing an ordinary resolution means that a simple majority of the votes cast at the meeting (for which proper notice was given) were in favour of the resolution. This does not change the rights of the shareholders - voting control and rights on a winding up are to remain the same.

Voting. A vote is taken in accordance with the company's Articles of Association. Generally it is by a show of hands. A declaration by the Chairman that the resolution is carried on a show of hands is all that is required to pass the resolution. The number of votes for and against do not need to be counted. When the resolution is passed the company is bound by it. So the resolution and the fact that it is passed should be recorded in the minutes of the meeting, taken by the company secretary.

STEP 3. FILING A COPY OF THE RESOLUTION AT COMPANIES HOUSE

A copy of every resolution must reach Companies House within 15 days of being passed. There is no filing fee for this.

To identify the resolution we recommend putting on it the company name, registration number, a heading of "Ordinary Resolution" and saying *"At an EGM of the above named company held at [place of meeting] and on [date of meeting] the following resolution was duly passed as an ordinary resolution..."* We also recommend that this copy of the resolution be signed by the Chairman as evidence of its authenticity.

Fast track (for private companies)

Written resolutions. You can do all this in writing, without anyone having to be notified of or turn up to a meeting, by using the statutory written resolution procedure. The resolution is passed by getting "unanimous" (100%) agreement to it by the members in writing. The signature of each member does not need to be on a single document, so the date the resolution is passed is the date on which the last member signs up to it. You will still need to file a copy of the resolution with Companies House within 15 days. Again, there is no filing fee for this.

> **Warning! Shareholders must agree to the split of dividends each year** – either in a general meeting or by using the written resolution method.

Sources

Share Capital and Prospectus (GBA6) and Resolutions (GBA7), both obtainable from Companies House website (www.companieshouse.gov.uk).

© PROFIT EXTRACTION, Indicator

APPENDIX 4: BONUS VERSUS DIVIDEND

SECTION 1: INTRODUCTION

Clearly money is required for living expenses and personal requirements, but before you decide to take out bigger sums you should consider:

- Whether there are sufficient funds available for the company to trade and grow as planned.

- What the tax implications are – corporate and personal.

- How to extract the money – although there are many options the most common methods are through payment of bonus or dividend. But how do they compare?

We've looked at these two methods separately in earlier chapters (Part 1 Bonus and Part 2 Dividends). Here we make a head-to-head comparison, also taking into account the various Corporation Tax implications.

SECTION 2: YOUR COMPANY

TAX-DEDUCTIBLE FOR THE COMPANY?

Bonus. A bonus paid is, in principle, always deductible for the company, as it is an expense wholly and exclusively incurred by the company for the purposes of its trade.

Dividend. The dividend is paid out of the company's profits after the tax due has been deducted. It is, therefore, not tax-deductible.

WHAT IS THE NI COST?

Bonus. The company has to pay employers' NI on your bonus at the rate of 12.8%. For example, a £10,000 bonus means the company has another £1,280 (12.8% x £10,000) to pay out.

Dividend. There is no employers' NI on it.

DOES THE COMPANY HAVE TO DEDUCT ANY TAX AND NI?

Bonus. The company must deduct income tax and employees' NI under Pay As You Earn (PAYE) from the bonus, and pay over the employers' NI due on it.

Dividend. The company should not deduct tax when paying a dividend. It is not a payment of earnings so it must not be included in payments subject to the PAYE system. Dividends are not subject to any class of NI.

Tax credit. Although no tax is deducted from the payment of a dividend, you do receive a dividend with a tax credit of one ninth of the net dividend attached. The shareholder is taxed on the gross amount of the dividend including the tax credit, but is able to use that tax credit to offset some or all of the tax due. The tax credit is not related to the Corporation Tax (CT) paid by the company.

ANY RESTRICTIONS ON PAYING EITHER?

Bonus. In principle you can withdraw as much profit by way of bonus as you want. It is counted as part of your total pay and there is no upper limit to this. Of course you cannot award more bonus than the company has in profits.

Dividend. A company can pay a dividend if it has made a profit (that is not cancelled out by losses). The profit figure considered is that amount left after Corporation Tax has been deducted. The maximum dividend payable by the company is an amount equal to the profit after tax for the year, plus any profits made in earlier years that have not been paid out.

DOES THE LEVEL OF COMPANY PROFITS MATTER?

Yes. The rates of Corporation Tax depend on the level of profits so the value of the tax deduction you get for a bonus will vary.

SECTION 3: YOU

WHAT IS THE NI COST?

Bonus. Bonus payments are subject to employees' NI at the following rates:

EMPLOYEES' NI ON A BONUS	
BONUS	**2005/06 RATES**
TOTAL EARNINGS BETWEEN £4,895 AND £32,760	11% *(OR 9.4%)**
TOTAL EARNINGS OVER £32,760	1%

The lower rate of NI for the middle band of earnings is paid if you are a member of an approved company pension scheme that provides certain minimum benefits on retirement and you have "contracted out" of the State Earnings Related Pension Scheme (SERPS).

Dividends. There is no employees' NI on dividends.

AT WHAT RATE WILL YOU BE TAXED?

The rate at which you pay income tax on your salary depends on the type and the grand total of your income during the tax year.

Bonus. The income tax rates for earnings in the tax year 2005/06 are:

INCOME TAX ON A BONUS	
TAXABLE INCOME	**TAX RATE**
ON FIRST £2,090	10%
ON NEXT £30,310	22%
ABOVE £32,400	40%

© PROFIT EXTRACTION, Indicator

Dividends. The income tax rates that apply to dividends received in 2005/06 are:

INCOME TAX ON A DIVIDEND	
TAXABLE INCOME	**TAX RATE**
ON FIRST £32,400	10%
ABOVE £32,400	32.5%

Tax already paid? The tax credit on your dividend voucher does not represent all the income tax to be paid to the Taxman. The credit is just a device to ensure that shareholders who only pay tax at 10% or 22% do not pay any further tax on the dividends they receive, but if you pay tax at 40% there is more to pay.

SECTION 4: EXAMPLE

This is an example of the tax-related consequences of withdrawing all of your profit as a bonus rather than a dividend.

We first look at what the company must pay in Corporation Tax to have net profits available to pay the dividend. We will then calculate the net amount that you will be left with as an individual after deduction of income tax.

We have used the following *assumptions:*

1. Corporation tax rates are those shown in section 2 for 2005/06

2. Income tax rates are those shown in section 3 for 2005/06

3. NI rates and bands are those announced for 2005/06

4. Your tax-free personal allowance has already been used elsewhere against another source of income

5. You start with a taxable profit of £70,000

So how much dividend or bonus can the company pay you?

COMPANY'S TAX POSITION		
2005/06	**BONUS METHOD (£)**	**DIVIDEND METHOD (£)**
TAXABLE PROFIT	70,000.00	70,000.00
LESS BONUS *(£70,000 / 112.8 x 100)*	-62,506.74	
LESS EMPLOYERS' NI ON BONUS *(£70,000 /112.8 x 12.8)*	-7,934.26	
TAXABLE PROFIT	-	70,000.00
CORPORATION TAX PAYABLE *(23.75% AND 19%)*	-	-13,300.00
POST-TAX PROFIT	-	56,700.00
LESS DIVIDEND		-56,700.00
RETAINED PROFIT	-	-

APPENDICES

YOUR TAX POSITION		
2005/06	**BONUS METHOD (£)**	**DIVIDEND METHOD (£)**
INCOME BEFORE TAXES	62,506.74	63,000.00
INCOME TAX AT 10%	-209.00	-3,240.00
INCOME TAX AT 22%	-6,668.20	-
INCOME TAX AT 32.5%	-	-9,945.00
INCOME TAX AT 40% *(ON EXCESS OVER £32,400)*	-12,042.70	-
LESS TAX CREDIT ON DIVIDEND *(1/9 x £56,700 = £6,300)*		6,300.00
TOTAL INCOME TAX	-18,919.90	-6,885.00
EMPLOYEES' NI	3,362.62	-
TOTAL DEDUCTIONS	22,282.52	-6,885.00
NET AVAILABLE TO SPEND	40,224.22	56,115.00

TOTAL TAX COST (COMPANY AND YOU)		
2005/06	**BONUS METHOD (£)**	**DIVIDEND METHOD (£)**
COMPANY TAX COST	7,934.26	13,300.00
YOU	22,282.52	6,885.00
TOTAL TAX COST	30,216.78	20,185.00
OVERALL TAX RATE ON PROFIT *(TOTAL TAX COST/PROFIT X 100)*	(£30,216.78 / £70,000) x 100 = 43.17%	(£20,185.00 / £70,000) x 100= 28.84%

© PROFIT EXTRACTION, Indicator